Gill & Macmillan Ltd
Hume Avenue
Park West
Dublin 12
with associated companies throughout the world
www.gillmacmillan.ie

© 2006 Bee Walsh & Jill Walsh

ISBN-13: 978 0 7171 4064 0
ISBN-10: 0 7171 4064 4

Photographs by Jill Walsh
Index compiled by Cover to Cover

Book design and typesetting by Graham Thew
Illustrations by Lynn Nalty
Colour reproduction by Typeform Repro, Dublin
Printed by GraphyCems Ltd., Spain

1 3 5 4 2

Contents

Introduction

bee:

On a visit to the United States in the 1960s, I came across the idea of summer activities for young people. From that, I commenced teaching a small group of teenagers how to cook light and easy meals. Broadening the palates of Irish people became my mission.

To take on this project during a time when Ireland was still partial to the burgers and chips diet, I felt I needed the best ammunition possible. I embarked on getting as many qualifications and life experiences as possible in foreign culinary skills. During the winter months, I taught home economics, and I spent many summers experiencing the culinary delights of the US and European countries, bringing back unusual ingredients and ideas. The Busy Bee summer school was born and grew from strength to strength. Foreign ingredients became readily available, and many summer schools followed in my footsteps. My mission became easier and, with the encouragement of my daughter Jill, I would like to pass on all the best recipes in the world. This book is aimed at anyone over 14 with a taste for good food and enjoyment of cooking.

jill:

Growing up in my house was a little different. Mum always had her head in a pot of unusual concoctions, experimenting with strange ingredients and mad combinations. Many of my friends were made to try her latest inventions as I went through my rebellious phase of eating frozen pizzas, red-faced at my mum's constant barrage of force-feeding my guests.

They tried to talk me round—'Your mum's an amazing cook', 'You're so lucky', 'I'd love to have dinners like that'. When most teens were taking their mums to clothes shops, my mum was making me sit through lavish lunches on the restaurant circuit. We struck a deal that I would drag her around the clothes shops in return for no refusals at the 'taste this' tables. Like a stubborn herb, I was ground down. It started with the éclairs, then the chocolate mousse—she went for my weak spots.

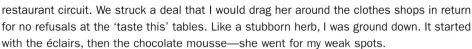

Soon the orange and ginger soup crept in, followed by the paella. I was hooked—there was no going back. I waved goodbye to fast food and went all out, learning from her how to conjure up a delicious meal out of a few ingredients. Mum's talent in the kitchen is endless. Bee truly has a unique talent of making the most complex dishes look easy. Together we wanted to share all her wealth of experience and knowledge of food. To make it easy, we have listed in the book all the farmers' markets nationwide from which you can buy your bounty. We hope you enjoy.

Utensils guide

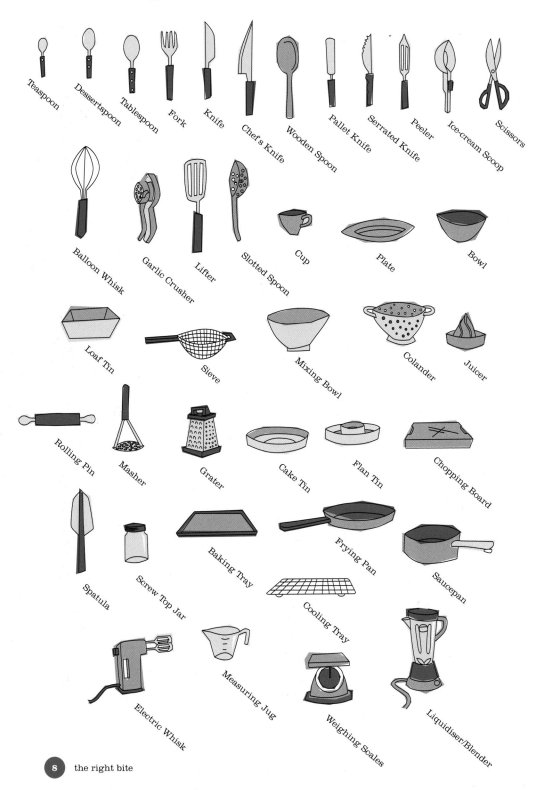

Teaspoon

Dessertspoon

Tablespoon

Fork

Knife

Chef's Knife

Wooden Spoon

Pallet Knife

Serrated Knife

Peeler

Ice-cream Scoop

Scissors

Balloon Whisk

Garlic Crusher

Lifter

Slotted Spoon

Cup

Plate

Bowl

Loaf Tin

Sieve

Mixing Bowl

Colander

Juicer

Rolling Pin

Masher

Grater

Cake Tin

Flan Tin

Chopping Board

Spatula

Screw Top Jar

Baking Tray

Frying Pan

Saucepan

Cooling Tray

Electric Whisk

Measuring Jug

Weighing Scales

Liquidiser/Blender

Acknowledgments

Bee:

This book is a grateful acknowledgment to all my past students who have, through their amazing intellect and interest in cooking, encouraged and amazed me through the years. My daughter Jill I cannot thank enough for all her input and pushiness. Thank you to Michael Gill and Alison Walsh for their faith in this project and giving us the catalyst for this book. To James at Cavistons for his endless knowledge of seafood. To Ken, my favourite butcher, for his meaty know-how. Special thanks to David Cassidy for his encouragement.

To Caitríona and Hayley for their ongoing support. To Aimeerose, Fionn and Niall for allowing their home to be monopolised in the research, and finally to Aylmer, Alan and Tara for their silent approval and always being there.

Jill:

To Alison Walsh, thank you for your encouragement and confidence; to Michael Gill for your support and creative freedom. To Mairead, Aoileann, Nicki, Emma and everyone else in Gill & Macmillan for adding their own ingredients along the way.

Thank you to Sheenagh Barron for her English skills and kitchen knowledge. Thanks to Ann and Liam for letting me swipe their camera for months on end. To Lynn Nalty for her fab illustrations. Thank you to Meadows & Byrne, Dún Laoghaire, and Storehouse, Dún Laoghaire, for the loan of their delph and kitchen equipment.

Thank you to Audrey and Peter O'Toole for letting us invade their new kitchen. Thank you to my gorgeous children, Fionn and Aimee rose, who were banned from the computer 'for ages'. Thank you to Tanya and Viv for your enthusiasm—two of my VBFs. Finally, thank you to my husband, Niall, for his continued support and patience.

Ratatouille

kitchen tips

An A to Z of culinary know-how

Aldente

This is a term which was originally used to describe when pasta or rice was just cooked. *Aldente* means right to the bite— not too soft or too hard. It is now also used when describing how vegetables should be cooked.

Allergies

Some people have food allergies, while others have food sensitivities. A *food allergy* is a serious, possibly life-threatening reaction to a particular type of food. Common foods that cause allergies are nuts, shellfish and summer fruits, such as strawberries or raspberries. Always find out whether any of your diners have known food allergies, as even a trace of the offending food could be very dangerous. Most restaurants nowadays post disclaimers on their menus regarding the possibility of nuts being present in their food, because the allergic reaction to nuts can be so very dangerous. Something as simple as a little sesame oil used in a stir-fry could be enough to cause a bad reaction. In the case of people with nut allergies, it is best to err on the side of extreme caution. Perhaps discuss with them ahead of time the recipe you are planning to use, so that they can inform you of any potential risks. With *food sensitivities,* a person has an adverse but not life-threatening reaction to certain types of food. Always ask your guests before planning your menu whether they have any allergies or sensitivities so that you can plan accordingly.

Allspice

This is obtained from a small berry found in tropical South America. It is often said that it is a mixture of cloves, cinnamon and nutmeg. However, while it has a smell reminiscent of all three, it is in fact not a mixture but a spice in its own right. Allspice is said to aid the digestive processes and is often used in desserts.

Apples

There are many varieties available to choose from. Pick bright, firm fruit without bruises. Apples are cleansing, aiding in the removal of impurities from the liver. They aid digestion and are a good source of vitamin C. Once cut, apples quickly begin to turn brown. This is a result of the oxidisation process and does not mean that the apples are bad or inedible. To prevent browning of apples, squeeze or brush a little lemon juice over them after you cut them.

Apricots

Delicious when fully ripe, gold and full of juice, these are used in a variety of sweet dishes. They can also be used to give a little boost of sweetness when sliced into salads. They are a good source of beta-carotene, vitamin A and fibre.

Asparagus

This is a delicate and delicious vegetable. To cook, place in boiling, lightly salted water for 3 to 5 minutes, then remove. Either serve immediately or cover immediately with cold water to keep the colour, retain the vitamin content, and to prevent it from becoming mushy. It can be very successfully reheated using the microwave. Traditionally it is served with hollandaise sauce or with a knob of butter melted over the top. It can also be roasted, rubbed over with a little olive oil and a sprinkling of sea salt. It is a rich source of vitamin C and has some laxative effects.

Aubergine

Also known as eggplant, this dark purple, glossy-skinned fruit is quite versatile. Choose glossy-skinned fruit, small or medium-sized, with no wrinkling to the skin. They can be stored in the fridge for up to two weeks. The firm skin makes them ideal for stuffing then baking with a variety of savoury fillings. The flesh is often used in casseroles or tomato-based sauces. Aubergine can be sliced with the skin on and baked rubbed over with olive oil and garlic and a sprinkle of sea salt. It is a good source of vitamin C and iron and potassium.

Avocados

These are best used when slightly soft to the touch. Often they are hard when purchased and may be ripened by placing at a window for a couple of days. They have a high fat content, but it is mono-unsaturated fat and therefore one of the healthy fats for anyone watching their cholesterol. They are usually served raw and have myriad uses. Avocados should be rubbed over with a little lemon juice as, if they are to be exposed to the air for more than a few minutes, they will begin to turn brown quickly.

Bake blind

When a recipe asks that something be baked blind, usually it is referring to the preparation of pastry. Take the pastry shell and place a piece of greaseproof or bakewell paper on the bottom of the inside of it. Then fill the shell up with dry kidney beans, and place in a moderate oven. The purpose of the beans is to prevent the pastry from puffing up or burning, but it is not absolutely necessary to fill the shell with them. We keep a jar of kidney beans to use only for the purpose of baking blind, and we would recommend this if it is something that you find yourself doing regularly.

Bakewell paper

This is used mostly in the preparation of meringues and pavlovas. Greaseproof paper can be used in most instances, but meringues will stick to it, so bakewell is preferred.

Bananas

Highly nutritious and versatile, bananas are applauded for varied health-giving benefits. They are rich in fibre, vitamins and minerals—in particular potassium—and are a healthy source of sustained energy. Bananas contain the amino acid tryptophan, which is thought to lift the spirits and aid sleep. They are used widely in cooking both savoury and sweet dishes, as well as in smoothies, ice-cream and frozen yoghurt.

Beans

Beans are the edible seeds from plants and there is a huge variety available. Many types of beans can be purchased in tinned form, which is okay but less desirable than preparing your own. To prepare and cook beans from their 'raw' state, you must soak them in cold water for at least 24 hours and then boil them for a minimum of 1 hour before consumption. Beans are renowned for their nutritious value and are packed full of protein, vitamins, minerals and fibre. Beans are often blamed for causing gas and bloating—to minimise this effect, use the following tips when preparing them:

- Change the water a few times during soaking, replacing it each time with fresh cold water.
- Never cook beans in the same water in which they were soaked.
- Skim off any 'scum' that forms on the surface of the water during boiling.
- Add a little dill, ginger or caraway to the cooking water to lend their pro-digestive qualities to the cooked beans.

Beef

Ireland is considered to be one of the best beef producers in Europe. All that green grass is good for the cows, giving us delicious cuts of beef. The most common cuts used are fillet, sirloin, strip loin, T-bone, rib steak and round steak. Minced beef comes from round steak. Always buy lean mince. When cooking a steak, leave the fat on for flavour and remove it once the beef is cooked.

Blanch and refresh

This means to cook a food item in boiling, lightly salted water for a few minutes, then remove it and immediately immerse it in cold water. In the case of vegetables, this cooking practice ensures that the colour of the vegetable is retained, as well as an optimum amount of its vitamins and minerals. To reheat, either pour over with hot water or microwave for a few seconds until heated through.

Breadcrumbs

Breadcrumbs can be bought or prepared at home. Use plain, white sliced pan and blend it in the liquidiser until the desired texture is reached. It is better to use two- or three-day-old bread, as the fresher stuff tends to clump up more. To make breadcrumbs for coating items that are to be deep fried, it is best to use very fine breadcrumbs. To make these, simply liquidise for a longer time, then put the breadcrumbs through a wide-gapped sieve. The leftover breadcrumbs that would not go through the sieve can be frozen and used later. These are ideal for dishes that call for the breadcrumbs to be mixed through the other ingredients (e.g. hamburgers or crab cakes) or sprinkled on top (e.g. deep-dish bakes where breadcrumbs and cheese are used to make a crispy topping).

Broccoli

Choose broccoli that has bright compact florets. Any sign of yellowing or a limp stalk means that it is past its prime. Trim the stalks off and preserve the florets. When peeled and diced, the stalks can be used in stir-fries and also in soups and stocks. Serve raw in salads or cook by placing in boiling water on high heat for 5 minutes. Drain and place in cold water to retain the bright green colour and to preserve the vitamin content. To reheat, simply pop in the microwave or pour over with boiling water. Shake excess water from the florets as they act like a sponge for fluids. They are also ideal for use in stir-fries and do not need to be pre-cooked for this. Broccoli is a member of the cruciferous family and has been shown to contain sulphur compounds which stimulate the production of anti-cancer enzymes, which inhibit the growth of tumours. Raw broccoli contains as much calcium as milk and also a good amount of vitamins B and C, as well as iron, zinc and potassium.

Cabbage

This is another vegetable that has become unpopular through misuse, which typically means overcooking! Cabbage is best eaten raw. White and red cabbages are delicious in salads, while savoy cabbage, with its crinkly leaves, is ideal for stuffing with savoury fillings. Cabbage has antibacterial and antiviral qualities, which makes it particularly effective against colon cancer and cancer of the breast and uterus. It is a good source of vitamins C and E, as well as beta-carotene, potassium and fibre.

Cake tins

There are many different types of cake tin available. Traditional tins, such as the Yorkshire tin, were and are produced using imperial measurements of inches. With the changeover to the metric system, these measurements have changed. At the moment, there is a vast array of sizes, all of which are not the exact same. Here is a brief list of the most commonly used tins, their names and respective measurements in both imperial and metric denominations:

Sandwich tins: usually used in pairs for a double-layer chocolate cake, etc. These are round tins and come in sizes of 17 cm ($6^3/_4$ in), 19 cm ($7^1/_2$ in) and 21 cm ($8^1/_2$ in).

Flan tin: this is a round tin with an indentation in the middle. The ideal size is 22 cm ($8^3/_4$ in) for a 2-egg sponge.

Loose-based tins: suitable for cheesecakes, these come in a size of 22 cm ($8^3/_4$ in) x 7 cm ($2^3/_4$ in) high. For a heavier cake, such as a wedding or Christmas cake, a 22 cm ($8^3/_4$ in) x 12 cm ($4^3/_4$ in) high tin is the best option.

A loaf tin comes in various sizes and is used mostly for bread and carrot cake. Always try to buy the best you can afford—the non-stick ones last longer and do not rust.

Cardamom

Cardamom comes in a pod or in powdered form. The pod gives a better overall flavour than the powder, but either is acceptable. If you are using the pod, you will need to remove the outer husk and grind the inner seed with a pestle and mortar. Cardamom is used widely in Indian cuisine and is said to be good for the relief of colds and coughs, as well as being beneficial to the digestive system.

Carrots

Full of vitamin A and the antioxidant beta-carotene, good-quality carrots are available most of the year. It is best to buy organic carrots as a large amount of the pesticides used is absorbed into the flesh. Another bonus is that organic carrots do not need to be peeled! Always remove the green feathery tops after purchase, as this draws the moisture away from the flesh of the carrots, making them less juicy.

Cauliflower

Choose cauliflowers that are still encased in bright green leaves. Serve raw in salads or cook by placing in boiling water on high heat for 8 minutes. Drain and place in cold water to preserve the vitamin content. To reheat, simply pop in the microwave or pour boiling water over it. Shake excess water from the florets as they act like a sponge for fluids. They are also ideal for use in stir-fries and do not need to be pre-cooked for this. Cauliflower is bitter and unpleasant when overcooked, which it often is. If you are not a fan of this vegetable, give it another go—try cooking it for less time and serving with a nice cheese sauce made by adding cheddar to a plain béchamel sauce. Cauliflower contains vitamin C, foliate and potassium. It also has a laxative effect!

Cayenne pepper

This fiery spice comes from the ground-down pod and seed of the chilli pepper, capsicum. It should be used sparingly as a little goes a long way. Always follow the recipe amounts carefully.

Celery

This versatile vegetable can be used in a variety of dishes and can be obtained all year round. It is delicious raw or in salads. It can be used sliced thinly into stir-fries, or lightly cooked in boiling salted water for 8 minutes, then drained. Most commonly used in casseroles, stews, soups and stocks, it is low in calories and rich in vitamin C and potassium.

Cheese

There is a wide variety of cheeses available and most of the recipes contained in this book specify which type to use. If you want to substitute one cheese for another in a recipe, as a rule of thumb try to swap like for like. For example, cheddar cheese in a recipe could be substituted with Edam or Gouda or another waxy yellow cheese, but could not be exchanged for Brie or feta or goat's cheese which are more curd-type cheeses. Nutritionally all cheese contains valuable amounts of calcium and protein, but the harder cheeses typically have a higher fat content, so eat them in moderation. However, it should be noted that goat's cheese has a higher fat content than many hard cheeses.
See also Parmesan cheese.

Chicken

Free-range chicken has the best flavour and the meat is firmer but free-range chickens are more expensive. Oven-ready chickens come in small, medium and large sizes. Always store chicken in the fridge, before and after cooking. When chicken is cooked and required for a salad, allow it to cool and then place it in the fridge. Chicken breasts are sold on their own and work out much more expensive to buy than whole chickens, simply because it can be a little tricky to remove the chicken from its carcass. Always use a chef's knife when cutting up a chicken. Some people wear rubber gloves because they don't like the feeling of raw meat.

Chilli peppers

There are more than 200 types of chilli pepper grown in the world! The red ones are not always necessarily hotter than the green ones, although this is often used as a rule of thumb for ascertaining strength. The heat in chillies comes from capsaicin which is found in the seeds, white membranes and, to a lesser extent, in the flesh. Usually the more seeds and membranes, the hotter the chilli will be. Therefore, bigger chillies tend to have milder flavour, while the smaller ones can be blisteringly hot. It is best to prepare chilli peppers wearing gloves as they can sometimes burn the skin and the juices will stay on the skin long after it has been washed. Dried chillies are usually stronger than fresh and are more readily available. Chilli powder is used quite a bit also but is less spicy than fresh or dried versions. Always stick to the amounts stated in recipes—even a small bit extra can make a spicy dish inedible! If you do wish to make something hotter, add tiny amounts at a time and taste test until you have reached your desired heat. Remember that chillies in hot food continue to release their heat for 24 hours after cooking, so a good rule of thumb is to make it a third less hot than you would like at the cooking stage. Chillies stimulate the release of endorphins ('feel-good' chemicals) in the body and are a useful decongestant for anyone suffering from sinus trouble. They are rich in vitamin C and beta-carotene. But be careful as too much chilli can also irritate the stomach!

Chocolate

Once considered a luxury, chocolate is available in many forms today. The richness of the chocolate is determined by the percentage of cocoa it contains. Most cooking chocolate has a low cocoa content and a high cocoa-butter content, making it easier to manipulate for cooking purposes. The traditional and most foolproof method of melting chocolate is to place it in a glass bowl on top of a saucepan of water that has been brought to the boil then turned down low enough for it to be steaming but not boiling furiously. Allow the chocolate to melt slowly, and remove it from the heat once all of the lumps have disappeared. A quicker way to melt chocolate is by placing it in a microwave-proof dish (not plastic) and microwaving it on the defrost setting for a minute or so, checking it all the time. It is easy to burn chocolate this way, so be vigilant! The recipe for chocolate mousse requires the use of Bourneville or other dark eating chocolate. It is recommended that the first method given for melting is used in this instance, as confectionery chocolate has a lower melting point than cooking chocolate.

Cinnamon

This well-known spice is available ground or in sticks. It is most commonly used in the powdered form as the sticks are too difficult to powder at home. Cinnamon is used in both savoury and sweet dishes and is renowned as an anti-bacterial detoxifier and cleanser.

Clothing

Try to be practical when considering what clothing to wear when cooking. The big no-nos in the catering industry are sandals, short pants and sleeveless T-shirts. In the event of an accidental drop or spill, the less skin exposed, the better are the chances of avoiding serious injury. It is recommended that an apron or bib be worn when preparing food, long hair be tied back neatly, and that the tea towel be hung from the belt of the apron rather than over the shoulder.

Cloves

Cloves are the unopened buds of a tree found in Asia and are commonly coupled with cinnamon as a spice used in the preparation of desserts. Clove oil is used as a remedy for toothache, and it is commonly thought to have antiseptic and anaesthetic qualities.

Cookie cutter

These are widely available in a variety of different sizes and shapes. The metal ones are most durable and versatile. When you are cutting out cookies or scones, simply dip your cutter into some loose flour in between cutting each item out of the dough. This makes for a clean cut and smoother edges on your finished product.

Coriander

This comes in powdered form as a spice or in fresh form as a green leafy herb that looks very similar to parsley. It has a very unique flavour and can be used chopped through salad to give it an extra lift. It is sometimes referred to as cilantro, though mostly in the US. Most recipes will specify, as ours do, whether the powdered or fresh form is required. They are not interchangeable within a recipe as the powdered form will not produce the same effect as the fresh, and vice versa. Ground coriander is obtained by toasting and grinding the seeds of the plant and is a central ingredient of most curries. Coriander is said to relieve digestive upset and nausea.

Corn

Fresh corn on the cob is best served boiled in lightly salted water for 15 to 20 minutes, then drained and rubbed over with a little butter. Baby corncobs are ideal for use in stir-fries or for eating raw in salads. Frozen corn is precooked and can be used in risottos, pilaffs, soups and stir-fries. Corn is a good source of vitamins A, B and C, as well as iron, magnesium, potassium and phosphorus.

Courgette

The smaller, the more flavourful is the key to picking good courgettes. They should be used within a few days of purchase. The skin should be bright green and glossy, and the flesh creamy in colour. Courgettes have a delicate flavour and are ideal for stir-fries. They can also be used very effectively sliced into salads. They can be cooked by steaming lightly but are least tasty this way. These vegetables are also delicious when rubbed over with olive oil and garlic and roasted for a few minutes. Do not cook for too long as they easily become mushy and tasteless. Courgettes are sometimes referred to as zucchini.

Cous cous

While it looks like a grain, cous cous is, in fact, a type of pasta processed from durum wheat. It originates in North Africa and has become very popular in recent years. The type that is generally available in grocery stores is the quick-cooking variety, which simply needs to be soaked according to the directions on the packet.

Cream

While it should not be used lavishly or on a daily basis, it makes a delicious and rich addition to soups and sauces, as well as being commonly used as a traditional accompaniment for many desserts. Be careful when you are whipping cream as it can over-whip very quickly and then turns into curd (butter!) Keep your eyes on it all the time. For spreading purposes, leave the cream a little looser than if you intend to pipe it or use it as a pastry filling (in which case having it a little thick is desirable). The fat content of cream varies, so it is best to refer to its container for this information. Some alternatives to cream are crème fraîche, sour cream or Greek-style natural yoghurt. It is worth noting that sour cream does not substitute well in cooked dishes as it curdles at high temperatures, so it is advisable to use crème fraîche as an alternative. Also keep in mind the relative trade-off you are making by substituting cream with something else: sour cream contains about 20 per cent fat. Greek-style natural yoghurt contains about 10 per cent fat. Crème fraîche has about 35 per cent fat. Just make sure that the cost in flavour is worth the amount of fat content being saved!

Cumin

Used in many ethnic cuisines such as Indian, Mexican and African, cumin is roasted and then ground. If you purchase the seeds, it is advisable to roast them first, as otherwise they will give a bitter taste to your dish. Cumin is ideal for serving with beans as its good effects on the digestive system seem to offset those caused by the beans!

Cutting/Chopping boards

When washing wooden cutting or chopping boards, first wash in sudsy hot water, cleaning off any staining, then rinse well in cold water to close the pores in the wood and prevent the growth of bacteria on the board. Glass chopping boards have become popular, but are not ideal as they will dull the edges of your knives very quickly. It is good practice to use a different board for the preparation of meat from the one you use for vegetables. For any board or other object, including your hands, that has come into contact with raw garlic, rinse well first in cold water and soap, and only then in hot water. If you use hot water first, it will effectively cook the garlic into the object or your hands, making the odour almost impossible to remove.

Decorate

This means to enhance the overall presentation of a sweet dish by the addition of something. For example, you may decorate a bowl of plain ice-cream by adding a raspberry and a sprig of mint to the top. We have tried to give decorative tips with most of the recipes here, but don't be scared to experiment with different kinds of decoration. The addition of a drizzle of coulis on a dessert plate can make a plain dessert extraordinary! A little sprinkle of icing sugar over the top of a dessert can give it a little extra jazz. Or a blob of cream with a nice piece of summer fruit popped on top can do it as well. Be adventurous!

Dressings

Another name used for many dressings is vinaigrette. The original French dressing is always 1 part vinegar to 3 parts olive oil, French mustard, garlic and seasoning. Do experiment with all sorts of flavours. Throughout this book we show you how to make many different dressings. Try not to buy the bottled stuff—it really is a waste of money and the flavours are very processed.

Eggs

Highly nutritious and versatile, eggs have an infinite number of uses. The size of the eggs referred to in the recipes throughout this book is always large size A eggs, and free range are preferred. Eggs are better when used at room temperature but stored in the refrigerator. Remove eggs from the fridge 30 minutes before use. To check if an egg is fresh, place it in a bowl of water—if it sinks and lies on its side, it is fresh.

To separate eggs: Above a bowl or cup, crack the egg against a hard sharp edge along its middle. Now tip one side of the egg back into the upright position and pull the upper half off of the top. The whites should pour out either side of the upright shell, leaving the yolk in the bottom half. If you get some yolk or a piece of shell into the whites, simply use the empty shell half to scoop it out. The yolk or piece of shell will gravitate towards the shell, enabling easy removal! Always remember, when making meringues there can be no yolk whatsoever in the whites. It is the fat contained in the yolk that causes the whites to collapse.

Eggs have got a lot of bad press over the years for their possible contribution to raising cholesterol levels. Recent opinion on this topic is that eggs are not as bad for us as was once believed. Saturated fats are now blamed more for their role in raising cholesterol, and since eggs are low in saturated fats, they have been given a reprieve. Eggs provide important B vitamins as well as protein, vitamins A and D, iron and phosphorus, and their nutritional content is affected very little by the cooking process.

Egg wash

Egg wash is typically used to brush over the top of pastry to give it a shine and prevent it from having a floury appearance after cooking. To make egg wash, simply break an egg into a cup or bowl and add a tablespoon of milk or water, then whisk well with a fork. Brush over the pastry with a pastry brush immediately before cooking.

Flour

There are myriad varieties of flour available. Typically when a recipe refers simply to 'flour', it means plain white flour. Self-raising flour is simply plain white flour with baking powder (raising agent) added during processing. Durum wheat is a heavier flour than either of these and is used to make pasta; it has a longer starch molecule and therefore holds the pasta shapes more effectively than the lighter types. There are several different types of brown flour available and they vary from brand to brand, depending upon how processed the wheat is. Nutritionally speaking, the less processed the flour, the better it is for you.

Folding

This refers to mixing a set of ingredients together by using long, smooth, up-and-down strokes of a large spoon or mixing implement. It implies that the mixture should *not* be mixed around and around vigorously, but blended slowly and smoothly, using strokes down to the bottom of the bowl and then pulling back up to the top until the two ingredients are married uniformly.

Homemade hamburgers

Frying pan

To make an ordinary frying pan non-stick, simply coat the entire surface of the pan with salt and cook over high heat for a minute or two, then wipe the salt off well with a little kitchen paper.

Garlic

Garlic is indeed a wonder food! It is full of health-giving qualities as well as providing a subtle and highly distinctive flavour unlike anything else. Garlic is sold in bulbs and each individual segment of the bulb is called a clove. Most recipes call for the use of a number of cloves.

When a recipe calls for *crushed* garlic, it may be prepared as follows: remove the papery skin from the clove and cut off the yellow woody bottom piece. Place in a garlic crusher and mash out the white pulp.

When a recipe calls for *creamed* garlic, it should be prepared as follows: Remove the papery skin from the clove and cut off the yellow woody bottom piece. Take a good pinch of salt and place it on top of the garlic on a chopping board. Using the flat side at the very tip of a knife (a large chef's knife is best) mush and mash the garlic until it has reached a creamy consistency. If you use creamed garlic in a recipe, remember that when seasoning you should cut back the amount of salt accordingly.

Garlic is very pungent. A good tip for not letting yourself end up smelling of it is always to wash using cold water and soap first when cleaning utensils or your hands. Then clean a second time, using soap and hot water. Using hot water on garlicky hands or utensils effectively melts the oils containing the smell into your pores.

When buying garlic, the smaller the bulb, the better the flavour. It will keep for up to about two months in a dry, cool place. **Never keep garlic in the fridge!**

Garlic is lauded as having many health-promoting qualities: it is said to lower cholesterol, boost the immune system, lift your mood and have a calming effect.

Garnish

This means to dress up or enhance the overall appearance of a *savoury* dish by the addition of something. Many different things can be used to garnish a dish. Have fun and experiment with different types of garnish. For example, a sprig of parsley and a slice of lemon is a very common garnish for fish dishes, but you needn't limit yourself to just plopping them on the side of the dish—you can experiment by making interesting shapes with the lemon to enhance the overall presentation of your dish.

Gelatine

Gelatine is used in setting cold soufflés, fruits, vegetables and meat moulds. It is purely a setting agent and is totally tasteless. Gelatine must be dissolved carefully before use. The original gelatine was made by melting down the hooves of animals—yuck! The vegetarian substitute is made from seaweed and is called Agar Agar.

Ginger

This is available in powdered form but far superior results are produced when the fresh root is used. Ginger is used in both sweet and savoury dishes and is famous for its settling effects on digestive upset—in particular, nausea. When choosing fresh root ginger, pick pieces that are firm, thin skinned and unblemished. Store in a cool, dark place.

Grapes

There are various different types of grape available. They should always be washed before use, as they are routinely sprayed with fungicides and pesticides. They have a variety of uses. Serve with cheese, in salads or as dessert decorations. The skins can be removed by first scoring the skins then blanching them in boiling water for a few seconds, then peeling the skin away with a small paring knife. They are a good source of iron, potassium and fibre.

Gravy

An old-fashioned word, it covers a range of light sauces or jus. Originally gravy was made by combining a little cornflour with the juice of the meat, followed by a liquid such as stock. Now it can include all sorts of ingredients.

Greaseproof paper

This is a particular type of cooking parchment and is widely available in supermarkets everywhere. Typically you can use bakewell paper instead of greaseproof paper, but not vice versa.

Greasing tins

To grease a cake tin so that nothing will stick to it, melt a knob of butter or margarine, add a teaspoon of flour, stir well. Using a pastry brush, brush the mixture over the entire surface of the pan or tin you are using. To line a tin with greaseproof paper, trace the outline of the tin with a pencil on the paper and use a scissors to cut it out to fit. To get the paper to stick to the sides and bottom of the tin, put a little butter or margarine between the paper and the sides of the tin, to 'glue' them together. Never grease a tin when making meringues, as the oil will make them collapse. For this, always use bakewell paper.

Hot oven

This refers to an oven set between 180°C and 200°C (350°F and 400°F) or gas mark 4–6.

Kiwis

Kiwi fruit is ideal for decorating desserts, especially in the winter months when many other fruits are not available. Choose fruit that is neither too soft nor too firm to the touch. Check around the base of the stem end for slight softness but the fruit should otherwise be firmer. When you are using kiwi fruit in smoothies or when making coulis, it is best to remove the seeds as they cause bitterness. To remove the seeds, push the entire peeled kiwi fruit through a wire sieve until only the pith and seeds are left. Kiwi fruit is a good source of vitamin C.

Knives

It is important to have a few good knives for proper food preparation. We would recommend that you have at least one of each of the following: a chef's knife, a paring knife, a small knife and a serrated-edge knife, also known as a tomato knife. Never wash your knives in hot water, just a little lukewarm soapy water, and rinse off in cold. Never put knives into a sink full of water—it would be easy to forget that they are in there and then cut a hand. Keep knives in the sheaths in which they were purchased, or else a knife block or some other safe place. Do not keep them in the cutlery drawer as it would be easy to cut a hand when rooting around in there. Keeping them in a sheath or knife block also prevents the edges from becoming dulled from constant contact with other utensils. Sharpen your knives regularly—ask in your nearest kitchen-equipment supply shop and either they will have a sharpening service themselves or they will be able to direct you to where you could get them done.

Lamb

The meat from a sheep under one year old is known as lamb. Meat from an older sheep is called mutton. This is a cheaper cut and is often used in stews. The well-known lamb cuts are leg, shoulder, rack or fair end, cutlets, gigot chops, loin chops and the neck. Lamb is delicious with mint. A little mint jelly added to your lamb gravy transforms the dish.

Lemons

Lemons should be deep yellow in colour, firm and heavy, with no green on the skin. The thinner the skin, the juicier the flesh

will be, so avoid the larger waxier lemons and opt instead for smaller and smoother-skinned varieties. Lemons are renowned for their cleansing properties and are a good source of vitamin C. The outermost layer of the skin of lemons, like all citrus fruit, contains aromatic oils and is often used in both savoury and sweet dishes.

To *grate* a lemon, rub the entire surface of the lemon over the finest plate on your grater. Use only the yellow pieces of rind without any of the white pith. This is called zest.

When *juicing* a lemon, first pop it into the microwave for 10 to 15 seconds on high, then roll it all over a flat surface to obtain the maximum amount of juice from it.

Lettuce

See Lettuce Alone page 168 for a complete guide to lettuces.

Limes

Choose firm limes, heavy for their size, with as little yellow to their skins as possible, as this is a sign of deterioration. You can usually *substitute* lemons for limes and vice versa in most recipes. Just remember: use a little less lime than lemon when you are substituting, as limes have a sharper flavour. As with other citrus fruits, pick the smoother varieties with less indentation on the peel, as these have better flavour, more flesh and contain more juice. All citrus fruits are full of vitamin C.

To obtain zests of lime, either use a grater or, if you don't have a grater, use a peeler to peel some strips from the lime rind, then cut them into finer strips.
When juicing a lime, first pop it into the microwave for 10 to 15 seconds on high, then roll it all over a flat surface to obtain the maximum amount of juice.

Low oven

This refers to an oven set at about 120°C (325°F) or gas mark 3. Very low would refer to an oven set between 80°C (175°F) and 100°C (215°F) or gas mark 1. This would typically be used only for meringues.

Mangetout

Mangetouts, meaning 'eat all' in French, are delicious when either steamed or boiled in lightly salted water for 3 to 5 minutes. Drain, then place immediately into cold water. Reheat right before serving by popping in the microwave or pouring hot water over them. Serve with a knob of butter. They are also delicious in stir-fries and salads. Mangetouts are a good source of vitamin C and iron.

Mango

This fruit can range in colour from green to yellow and orange and red. The greener they are, the less ripe they are. They are ripe when soft but not mushy to the touch. They can be difficult to prepare as they have a large flat stone that is off-centre, and the flesh is slightly stringy, making it difficult to cut through. When you are using the fruit for most things, the best way to tackle it is to peel off the outer skin with a paring knife, removing as little of the flesh as possible, then simply slice away at the flesh until the stone is all that is left. However, if you need cubes of mango—in a fruit salad, say—it is best to cut the unpeeled fruit vertically down one side of the stone on either side, then cut away any flesh remaining around the stone. Taking the two large slices, and using a small sharp knife, cut the flesh into a criss-cross pattern. Now turn the mango upside down and, using a knife to pare away the skin, let the cubes come away as they will.

Margarine

Most of the recipes here specify whether to use soft or hard margarine. Typically you would use hard margarine in the preparation of pastry and soft margarine in the preparation of cakes and cookies. Hard margarine is purchased in a block form, usually covered with foil or greaseproof paper. Soft margarine is usually purchased in a plastic tub and is easy to scoop out. You can equally use butter in most of the recipes in this book, but it is worth noting that, while the debate continues regarding the health benefits of butter versus margarine, whichever you decide to use will often not make a significant difference to the flavour. Where it is specified that butter should be used, it usually means that you cannot substitute it with margarine without a significant trade-off in the resulting flavour.

Marinade

This means to flavour and to tenderise a particular food item before cooking it. Usually it involves preparing some kind of marinade (there are many types) and then immersing the food item (usually meat) to absorb the flavours over time. For meat, the process has the second function of tenderising the flesh before cooking. Marinades can also be used for vegetables and other foods. Most recipes will state how long to leave the food steeping in the marinade before further preparation or cooking.

Mayonnaise

We make our own, and most mayonnaise is made from eggs, olive or vegetable oil and a little acid like vinegar or lemon juice. Always keep mayonnaise in the fridge.

Measurements

1 oz is approximately equal to 25 g. $1/4$ pint is equal to 5 fluid ounces or approximately 150 ml.

Melons

Most varieties have a water content of over 90 per cent. Melons with orange-coloured flesh will have a higher vitamin C content. When purchasing, look for fruit that feels heavier for its size and that has a slight softness around the stem end but is otherwise firm to the touch. Melons are used widely in fruit and other salads. The seeds and pith should always be removed. For presentation purposes, it is well worth investing in a melon-baller to achieve nice uniform balls of melon. If you do not have one, use a teaspoon to scoop out little rounds of the flesh. Melon is often used as a starter or between courses as it helps to cleanse the palate and is not filling.

Meringues

Meringues are a simple and popular dessert item. When making them, there are a few important tips to remember:

- Never use a plastic bowl for making meringues as they will never reach their optimum volume.
- Always make sure that there is absolutely no yolk in the whites! The fat that is contained in the yolk will make the meringues collapse. This is why greaseproof paper is used and not a greased dish for meringues—any oil or fat coming in contact with them is disastrous!
- Always use an electric mixer on high. Whisk the egg whites until they stand up in stiff peaks. The old test for when the eggs are stiff enough is to turn the bowl upside down, and they do not spill out. Feel free to try this if you like, but be careful!
- Always add the sugar little by little, beating all the time. You will know the mixture is ready when it does not drip off the whisks.
- The only cooking meringues need is to be dried out completely—that is why they are cooked on such low heat and for so long. Long ago, people would put meringue overnight into a hot press or airing cupboard to 'cook' it!

Pavlova is simply meringue with some vinegar added—it is the addition of vinegar that creates the marshmallow-like centre associated with pavlova.

Moderate oven

This refers to an oven set at between 140°C (275°F) to 160°C (315°F) or gas mark 2.

Mushrooms

There are many varieties of mushroom available, the most commonly known of which is the button mushroom, usually found in supermarkets. Button mushrooms can be used raw in salads, or lightly cooked. When a recipe calls for mushrooms, it is assumed that this is the variety to be used, unless otherwise stated. Another common variety is the cap mushroom, which has a wide flat top with the brown gills very visible. This type is more suitable for use in cooked dishes and is delicious stuffed with savoury fillings and then baked.

To clean mushrooms, rinse under the cold tap and rub dry using kitchen paper. Do not allow them to soak as it will make them mushy. It is not necessary to peel mushrooms. Mushrooms are a useful source of B vitamins and iron.

Mustard

There are three different kinds of mustard seed—white, brown and black. Black has the strongest flavour of the three. Mustard can be purchased in powdered form, where it has been roasted and crushed, or in seed form. When using the seed form, it is advisable to make sure that the seeds are roasted before use. There are myriad different types of prepared mustard condiments available. The two used most often in this book are English mustard and Dalkey mustard, both of which are readily available and delicious. Feel free to experiment with other kinds though, especially when preparing salad dressings. Types to avoid in making dressings would be the tabletop bright-yellow mustards, which are more suitable for use on sandwiches, burgers, hot dogs, and the like.

Noodles

Noodles can be made from a variety of different grains including rice, wheat and mung-bean flours. Similar to pasta, noodles are low in fat and give a high delivery of complex carbohydrates that provide energy.

- *Wheat noodles* include such types as egg noodles, ramen noodles and udon noodles. Whole-wheat noodles are richer nutritionally but all noodles are a good source of both carbohydrates and protein. To cook noodles, place them in a large pan of boiling water and cook for 3 minutes or so (refer to packet as the thickness will vary the cooking time). Remove from the hot water and place immediately into cold water to prevent them from overcooking.

- *Rice noodles* come in a variety of sizes. They are always precooked so they should be soaked in hot water for only a few minutes to soften them—if you are in doubt, prepare according to the instructions on the packet.
- *Mung-bean noodles* are made from mung-bean starch and are usually translucent and commonly known as cellophane vermicelli. Mung beans are hailed as a wonderful detoxifier. They do not need to be boiled but should merely be soaked in boiling water for 10 or 15 minutes to achieve optimum consistency. They have almost no flavour and are unsuitable for serving on their own.

Nuts

There is a huge variety of nuts available. We will mention only the ones used in the recipes in this book.

- *Almonds* are available in most supermarkets, ready blanched and peeled whole, chopped or in powdered form. If you wish to use whole fresh almonds, you can peel them by boiling them in a little water for a few minutes— this will allow the skins to come away easily. To make ground almonds, peel them first, then simply place them in the food processor for several minutes until they are powdered.
- *Cashew nuts* are always sold removed from their outer casing as they are, in fact, the seed of a fruit. They are delicious in stir-fries or sprinkled over a salad.
- *Coconuts* have dense white meat and are used to produce coconut chips, desiccated coconut, coconut milk and coconut cream, all of which are high in fat and should be used in moderation. Coconut is used widely in a variety of sweet and savoury dishes.
- *Pecan nuts* have an appearance similar to walnuts but have a sweeter flavour, lending themselves to common use in desserts. They are almost always sold shelled. But be warned—they have the highest fat and calorie content of any nut!
- *Pistachio nuts* are a delicious nut most often served on their own as a snack food. Typically they are sold salted and in the shell. Use them to sprinkle over salads or crush them up as a dessert topping. They can also be used as an alternative to the pine nuts in pesto— just remember that if you are using the salted kind, no further seasoning will be necessary!
- *Walnuts* are available whole, chopped or ground and are used most commonly in sweet dishes. However, they are also delicious crushed into stir-fries or over salads, and our delicious alternative to the traditional pesto is a simple must-try recipe!

See also *Allergies*.

Oils

Typically the recipes in this book specify which type of oil to use in a given recipe. The healthiest oils are the monounsaturated oils, such as olive oil and sesame seed oil, which can help to reduce the harmful 'LDL' cholesterol. While these oils are used where possible, they are not always suitable as they are typically quite dense and heavy and their use may change the consistency of the dish if substituted in the place of a lighter oil. Other 'good' oils are the polyunsaturated kinds which include walnut oil, canola oil and soybean oil. They are an excellent source of the essential fatty acids, omega 3 and 6, whose benefits have received so much attention in recent years. Sunflower oil is rich in polyunsaturated fats and is the best all-round oil to use as it is light and virtually tasteless. For the deep-fat fryer it is recommended that you use either sunflower or vegetable oil. There is a huge variety of speciality oils available and these are either cold pressed from seeds or nuts or alternatively produced by infusing a bland oil like grape-seed oil with other flavours. These are fun to experiment with in salad dressings as they will give a different spin to the end result.

While it is important to watch your overall fat consumption, remember that a little of these things is considered an essential part of a healthy, balanced diet. Recent research points out that the health-giving benefits of HDLs and the omega 3-6-9 fatty acids that are found in many oils are not only beneficial but absolutely necessary for overall wellbeing.

Onions

There are many varieties of onion:

- *Red Onions* are sweet with a light flavour and are ideal for use in recipes calling for raw or light cooking.
- *Scallions* are smaller with long green stems, a portion of which can be used in cooking to lend colour. They have a light fresh taste and crispy texture. They are often used in Chinese dishes and salads.
- *Shallots* are used mostly in cooked dishes and sauces and are smaller than the common yellow onion.
- *Yellow onions* are the type most commonly used worldwide, and when a recipe calls simply for onion, this is the type being referred to. This type will keep for one to two months in a cool, dark place. **Never store onions in the fridge!**

Raw onions are thought to be good for the reduction of the bad LDL cholesterol. Cooked and raw onions are antibacterial and antiviral and help with colds, congestion, asthma and hay fever. To chop an onion finely and avoid crying in the process, follow these simple instructions: cut the whole onion in half, then remove the papery skin from each half. Cut off the top piece, leaving the hairy bit on. Now, using a small, sharp knife, make several cuts laterally and horizontally in the onion, then slice away from front to the hairy bit at the back—and *voilà* finely chopped onion with no tears!

Oranges

Oranges are full of vitamin C. To get most value from them, use them as quickly as possible after peeling. The outermost layer of the skin of oranges contains aromatic oils and is often used in both savoury and sweet dishes.

To obtain *zests* of orange, either use a grater or, if you don't have a grater, use a peeler to peel some strips from the orange rind then cut them into finer strips.

When *juicing* an orange, first pop it into the microwave for 10 to 15 seconds on high, then roll it all over a flat surface to obtain the maximum amount of juice.

Paprika

This is made from mild chilli peppers which are dried and then ground into powder. Paprika has a strong orange colour and a unique flavour that also adds heat. It is a milder cousin of cayenne pepper and, like cayenne, has antiseptic properties and, when taken in small amounts, is said to aid digestion.

Parmesan cheese

This cheese is renowned for its pungent smell and strong flavour which it attains by the lengthy maturation process of between 1 and 4 years that it undergoes before going to the marketplace. It is high in fat, but not as high as cheddar, and very little of it will impart an enormous amount of flavour. Avoid the ready-grated variety—it is a poor substitute for the real thing. Invest in a small grater, buy it in lump form and grate it yourself as it is needed. It stays fresh for a long time in the fridge, so there is no excuse that it will not get used up!

Pasta

Pasta is considered an important part of a healthy diet. It is a low-fat food that is a good source of complex carbohydrates which provide energy to the body. Most pasta is made from durum wheat which is stronger than plain white flour. Coloured and flavoured pastas are created by the addition of a variety of different ingredients, varying from tomatoes to spinach and even chocolate! Egg noodles are produced in a manner similar to pasta but with the addition of eggs. Where possible, use whole-wheat pasta to increase the nutritional value of the meal, but keep in mind that it will need to be cooked a little longer than plain pasta. To cook pasta: put the uncooked pasta into a pot with plenty of boiling, lightly salted water. Stir it regularly to prevent it from sticking, and leave the lid off. Boil it until it is *aldente* (that means until the pasta is soft but not mushy, firm but not hard). Drain the pasta in a colander and run the cold tap through it to wash off excess starch. If you are making pasta ahead of time, it can be preserved in a container of cold water and drained out when ready to use. Reheat using the microwave or by pouring hot water over it. Pasta will keep in the fridge for up to two days.

Pastry

This is such a massive topic that it would be impossible to cover even a small portion of everything that could be said, so we have shaved it down to the following:

- Use hard margarine or butter—soft margarine is much more difficult to work with and reduces your chances of having a successful end product.
- Keep it cold! The colder the flour, the margarine, the water, the work surface, your hands, the room, the better!
- Keep it in the fridge! Once pastry is prepared into a ball of dough, it is best to put it into the fridge for at least 30 minutes or until you are ready to use it. If there are any delays in it going into the oven, pop it back into the fridge or a cold room.
- Too wet? If your pastry has become too wet, simply add a little more flour to it, kneading it through well, and then reassess the situation. If it is still too wet, add a little more...
- Too dry? If your pastry is too dry and crumbly, you will need to add a little more cold water, making sure to work it through well with your hands until the dough makes a uniform ball that is neither wet nor crumbly.
- Flouring—when you are rolling out pastry, make sure to sprinkle a handful of flour over the surface area you are going to

roll it out on. Also rub a little flour over the entire surface area of the rolling pin itself. Re-flour the work surface as often as is necessary. If the dough begins to stick to the surface, simply dust a little more flour over it.
- Egg Wash—brush a little egg wash over the top of the pastry before putting it in the oven. This gives the cooked product a nice shine and eliminates the 'floury' look. You can even do this when you are using frozen vol-au-vent cases, to give them a nicer finished appearance.

Peaches

These range in colour from gold to deep red and are a summer fruit. Avoid buying overly ripe fruit. It is better to buy firmer fruit ahead of use and allow it to ripen. To speed up the ripening process of most fruits, you can place them in a brown paper bag with other already ripened fruit for a day or two. Most of the vitamin C is contained just under the skin, so it is best to eat with the skin. Peaches also contain the antioxidant beta-carotene which is beneficial to the eyes and skin. To remove the stone, cut around the middle of the fruit down to the stone using a small paring knife. Twist the two halves of the peach in opposite directions, then prise out the stone. Rub over with lemon juice to preserve it and prevent it from becoming brown.

Pears

As with most fruits, pears are best during their own season, which is in late summer and early autumn. To check whether a pear is ripe, feel around the base of the stalk which should be soft to the touch, and the rest of the surface should be firm. Pears have a short prime, lasting only a few days. They are a good source of vitamin C and, because of their high pectin levels, are thought also to be able to lower harmful cholesterol in the body.

Peas

These are one of the few vegetables that can be frozen very successfully. Defrost a handful in some cold water and add them to a salad in winter when salad vegetables are less available. They should be cooked very lightly in boiling water, then drained and served with a little butter and salt. They can also be used very successfully in risottos, pilaffs and stir-fries. They are a good source of vitamin C and iron.

Pepper

Pepper not only adds its own flavour to a dish, but also helps to draw out the flavours of the other ingredients. The use of a *black peppercorn* mill is recommended for all of our recipes. The only exception to the use of black pepper is for white sauces where it is more desirable to use *white peppercorns*, thereby avoiding black specks in the finished product. *Green peppercorns* are the mildest kind available and are sometimes used to make peppercorn sauces. Pink peppercorns are not actually a true pepper and are actually a berry from a type of poison ivy—they are slightly toxic and are best avoided.

Peppers

These are available in an array of colours: red, yellow, green, orange, even purple! Green peppers are actually a not fully ripe version of the others, and therefore have a slightly more bitter flavour and are sometimes more difficult to digest. All types can be stored for a week or longer once refrigerated. They are used widely in both hot and cold dishes. The stem, seeds and pith should always be removed. Occasionally a recipe will call for peeled peppers (sliced peeled red peppers are known as pimiento and are used in many Spanish dishes such as paella). To remove the skin from a pepper, cut it in half, place it on a roasting tray and roast it in a hot oven for 20 to 30 minutes until blackened and blistered. Remove and place in a plastic bag as the steam will encourage the skin to lift away from the flesh. Bell peppers are a good source of vitamin C, beta-carotene and some B complex vitamins.

Pineapple

Pineapples are one of the few fruits that do not ripen further after picking, so, when selecting, choose ones with fresh spiky leaves and that feel slightly soft to the touch. Store in the fridge.

Plums

Plums should be purchased when they are still quite firm to the touch and should be left at room temperature to become ripe. Once they have ripened, plums are better kept in the fridge to halt the ripening process. To remove the stone, cut around the middle of the fruit, down to the stone, using a small paring knife. Twist the two halves of the plum in opposite directions, then prise out the stone.

Pork

A white meat, pork is delicious. The pure form of meat from a pig, its most common cuts are leg, spare rib, shoulder and pork chops. The tenderloin is the leanest cut of pork. Pre-packed pork should last two to four days in the fridge. Always cook pork well.

Potatoes

There are dozens of varieties of potatoes and some are better than others for particular cooking methods. Small potatoes and new potatoes are best boiled. They are firmer and waxier and this makes them ideal for potato salads. Larger or old potatoes are more suited to roasting, baking or mashing or for making chips. Do not use potatoes that have green patches as this indicates the presence of toxic alkaloids called solanines. Potatoes are high in complex carbohydrates that provides sustained energy levels. They have both protein and fibre, together with vitamins B and C, as well as iron and potassium.

Pre-heating oven

It is best to turn on an oven approximately 5 minutes before use to ensure a good result.

Potato cubes with bacon & balsamic dressing

Raspberries

A summer fruit, they are delicious but fragile. Handle them as little as possible and wash only if absolutely necessary. They are a good source of vitamin C.

Rice

Rice is a valuable staple food that provides a steady supply of energy as well as vitamins and minerals. There are various different types of rice widely available nowadays. Long-grain white rice is often treated with preservatives or chalk to make it whiter so it is essential that rice be well rinsed before use. To rinse rice, place it in a fine sieve and pour cold water over it until the water runs clean. To cook it, use 1 cup of long-grain rice to 2 cups of cold water and place together in a saucepan. Heat until it boils then lower the heat and simmer for 10 minutes or until it

is *aldente* (this means until soft but not mushy, firm but not hard). Drain in a colander or sieve and run some hot water over the rice to wash off any extra starch. Shake well and leave it sit for a little while in the colander or sieve until all the water has drained away. Rice can be prepared ahead of time and preserved cold, then drained and reheated in the microwave very effectively. Be careful! Bacteria forms on cooked rice very easily, so if it is to be kept for more than an hour before use, it should be refrigerated. Always use cooked rice within 24 hours or discard. Some other popular types of rice are:

- *Jasmine rice* which has a mild perfumed flavour and is often used in Indian cooking
- *Basmati rice* which also has a unique aromatic and fragrant flavour and is also used more often with Indian dishes
- *Valencia rice* which is a short-grained rice

that is used in traditional Spanish paella
- *Risotto rice* which is used in Italian risotto because it absorbs more fluid than other varieties of rice, while still retaining its 'bite'
- *Sushi rice* which, not surprisingly, is most often used in the preparation of Japanese cuisine where it is mixed with rice vinegar to produce the sticky filling associated with sushi.

Saffron

This is the most expensive spice in the world! Only a very small amount is needed to give colour and flavour to a dish. It is made from the dried stigma of a particular variety of crocus. It is believed to be an aphrodisiac! Powdered saffron may also be used instead of the thread form, but a little more of the powder should be used when substituting.

Salt

Use a good sea salt in a grinder or mill. Be very careful when adding salt to dishes. Err on the side of under salting a dish rather than over salting. Remember that there will be salt on the table, so more can be added. You can always add a little more, but it is hard to take it out once it's in there!

Sauces

Sauce is a liquid that has been thickened by various means. For example, a roux is made with flour and butter. Egg yolks, cornflour, arrowroot and cream are also used as a thickening agent. Just reducing the liquid by simmering can thicken a sauce also.

Sauté

This means to fry without colouring the food. In other words, keep the heat at a level where the ingredients are softening out and cooking, but are not attaining any colour (e.g. browning).

Seeds

There is a huge variety of seeds available. The most popular are the following:

Sesame seeds are tiny white or black seeds that are used in a variety of ways in bread making, desserts and savoury dishes. It is easy to toast sesame seeds either in the oven or on a dry pan—just be vigilant as they burn easily!
Sunflower seeds, the seed of the sunflower, are a good source of vitamin E. They are ideal for use in bread-making, or roasted and sprinkled in salads and stir-fries.

Shellfish

This is an enormous topic to which we could not do justice within the confines of this book. There are a few important safety tips to remember when handling shellfish.
- Shellfish should always be purchased from a reputable fishmonger or supermarket and you should make sure to use it within 24 hours of purchase.
- Do not use if it has a strong fishy odour.
- Use only molluscs (clams, mussels etc.) that have opened during the cooking process—never prise a shell open and eat the contents.

Simmer

When any dish has come to the boil and then the heat is turned way down, usually to its lowest setting, it is said to be simmering. Dishes are simmered to allow the flavours of the food to disperse and the cooking process to be completed.

Soy sauce

This is made from wheat, soybeans and salt which are then cultured using a fermentation process that can take up to three years. There are two types of soy sauce available—light soy sauce, suitable for tabletop use and saltier than the other type; and dark soy sauce, typically used during the cooking process as well as for marinades and sauces.

Spinach

This has become popular again since its widespread use as a salad ingredient. It does not preserve well and so should be eaten within a couple of days of purchase. It is best used raw to preserve its many health benefits, but can also be delicious when boiled for a couple of minutes in hot water then drained quickly. Nutmeg is a traditional and delicious accompaniment to cooked spinach. Simply add a pinch and mix through the cooked leaves. Spinach is an excellent source of beta carotene and contains fibre, iron, vitamins C and B6, calcium, potassium, foliate, thiamine and zinc.

Stocks

Stock is water in which meat, fish or vegetables have been cooked. It is used as the base for soups sauces and gravies. For a meat stock, it is better to simmer for at least 1 hour. For fish, 15 minutes should suffice.

Strawberries

A summer fruit, these are best in Ireland in June and July, and while the Irish fruit is smaller in size than its imported rivals, there is absolutely no comparison in flavour. The Irish strawberry is in a league of its own for sweetness and juiciness. Strawberries are delicious served on their own and are a very useful decoration for almost any other dessert. Wash only if absolutely necessary and do so only immediately prior to serving. They are rich in vitamin C and the B complex vitamins and potassium.

Tomatoes

There are dozens of varieties of tomatoes. Common ones are the egg-shaped plum tomato, ideal for use in cooking, the vine tomato and cherry tomato, ideal for use raw on sandwiches or in salads. Look for deep red fruit with firm but yielding flesh. To ripen, place at a sunlit window or leave at room temperature for a couple of days until completely reddened. They are a good source of vitamin E, beta-carotene, magnesium, calcium and phosphorus. To peel a tomato, score the outside with a small knife, then immerse the fruit in boiling water for 4 minutes, remove and

place in cold water. Remove the skin by peeling away from the flesh. To remove the seeds, cut the tomato in half and scoop out the seeds with a knife. Tomato seeds can give sauce a bitter flavour—removing them and the skins will give you a smoother, sweeter end product.

Turmeric

This is obtained from the dried and powdered root of the turmeric plant. It is sometimes used as a substitute for saffron as it gives a yellow colour to dishes. It does, however, have a distinctly different flavour from saffron. It lends subtle spicy warmth to dishes and is used most commonly in Indian cooking. It is said to be an antibacterial that can aid digestive functions.

Vinegar

There are many different types of vinegar available. The basic types are as follows:
- *Wine vinegar* is made from red, white or rosé wine and varies in quality much the way wine itself does.
- *Balsamic vinegar* is made from grape juice and fermented for a long time. The quality will usually depend on the length of the fermentation.
- *Malt vinegar* is made from sour beer and is most commonly used for pickling other foods. It is not suitable for use in salad dressings as the flavour is too harsh.
- *Rice vinegar* is made, not surprisingly, from rice, and is used in the making of sushi rice, as it is bland and mellow.
- *Cider vinegar* is made from cider and has a sharper flavour than wine vinegar so should be used sparingly in the preparation of dressings.
- *Flavoured vinegars* are usually created by infusing one of the basic types with other ingredients. You can experiment with creating your own flavoured vinegars by infusing a good basic vinegar with a variety of things. Some suggestions for items that are suitable to infuse vinegar are: rosemary, tarragon, cinnamon sticks, whole peppercorns, whole chilli peppers, or garlic.

Wild rice

Wild rice is, in fact, not a true rice. It is an aquatic grass found in North America. It has a unique nutty flavour and lends colour and texture to otherwise plain rice dishes, from pilaffs to salad. Wild rice is very popular at present and can be obtained in most supermarkets. It takes longer to cook than other types of rice— you should follow the same directions as for other rice but allow it to simmer for 40 to 50 minutes after boiling.

Wire tray

This is a metal mesh tray that stands up and away from the surface underneath. It is used to cool baked items uniformly and to prevent the underneath portion from becoming soggy through the build-up of condensation when the hot item comes in contact with a cold surface. Almost all cakes and pastries will require being put on a wire tray once removed from the oven. All of the recipes here state whether it is necessary to use a wire tray—so if it doesn't say that one is needed, you may assume that it is not!

Yeast

Yeast is a biological raising agent used for making breads and pizza bases. To activate, it needs warmth, moisture and food. However, extreme heat kills the growth of yeast. Yeast is made by feeding yeast cells with sugar. A person with candida is said to have a sensitivity to yeast.

Zest

Zest is used for flavouring and decoration. It is obtained by grating the outer skin of most citrus fruits. If you grate into the pith, this makes it bitter. A narrow strip of peel is called julienne.

Zucchini

Zucchini is the name commonly used for courgette in the US and Canada.

Herb Top 10

There is no excuse not to have a herb garden. Basil, coriander and mint can be grown in small spaces, even indoors on a sunny windowsill. So, get out your soil and seeds. There are too many great herbs to mention so we have given you our top ten most frequently used herbs.

1. Garlic

Garlic is a cousin of the onion but it's actually a member of the lily family. It is the most versatile herb. As well as having a glorious flavour, garlic is incredibly good for you. It can lower blood pressure and cholesterol, as well as having anti-bacterial properties, and warding off vampires. There is a Garlic World in Gilroy, northern California—worth a visit if you are ever in that neck of the woods. We sampled everything from garlic chocolate to garlic ice-cream.

2. Coriander

Also known as cilantro, coriander is one of our favourite herbs. It is very like flat parsley in appearance but its distinct flavour leaves parsley in the dust. Traditionally used in Indian dishes, coriander is now enjoying a burst of popularity in salads and soups, even bread. It has a lemon scent and a citrus zesty flavour.

3. Basil

Basil has an oval soft leaf and it is famous in Italian cookery. The basis of pesto and the basic herb for thousands of new recipes, it's got to be the king of herbs. Try growing your own. Basil needs very little water and grows back if you behead it for your fresh pesto. There is also a purple variety.

4. Mint

A delicious sprig of mint can cool curries and be used in the conjuring up of raita. It grows and spreads like wild fire. Mint is delicious mixed with fruit or just on its own in a refreshing drink.

Bruschetta

Gambas pil-pil

Pasta pesto

Grilled guacamole nests with prawn and

Crunchy garlic mussels

Deep-fried camembert with red onion marmalade

Garlic mushrooms

Beef koftas

Minted & mellow

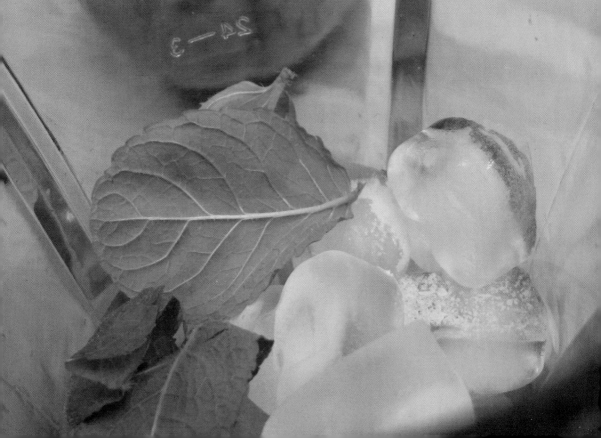

Cavistons Food Emporium

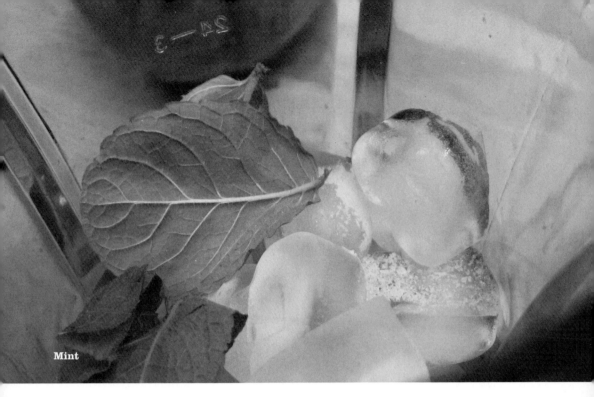

Mint

5. Fennel

Fennel can be used with pork, veal and fish, and is great in salad dressings. The seeds are used as a spice—they have a liquorice flavour and make a particularly good bread ingredient. Fresh fennel has a bulb-like appearance, not unlike garlic. Never plant fennel near coriander or dill, as they will grow poorly beside this herb.

6. Tarragon

Very popular in French cooking, tarragon is great with egg and cheese-based dishes. When using tarragon in cooked dishes, it is better to add it at the end, as heat tends to decrease its flavour. It has slender leaves and can be added to mayonnaises and salad dressings.

7. Parsley

There are two types of parsley. The flat leaf is mostly used in cooking and the curly type as a garnish. We don't find this herb very exciting but it is a good source of vitamin C, and chewing parsley after eating garlic is said to get rid of bad breath. Break out the chewing gum instead. Overused and out of date. Carry on.

8. Chives

A member of the onion family, chives are delicious and mega versatile. Chop them into salads and sauces or pop them into wraps. They make a great garnish and are easy to grow.

9. Rosemary

Wonderful and aromatic, rosemary is great with meat dishes. Use it in a marinade or freshly picked and smoked in your barbecue to give a great flavour. Its needle leaves make a great-looking plant.

10. Oregano

It's tops in tomato-based dishes. When fresh, oregano is full of robust flavour and is great in vinaigrette. Like tarragon, it loses its flavour quickly when cooked so should be added last to dishes. It has mint-like leaves.

So there they are—our top ten flavours. Cooking is a science, so don't be afraid to experiment with different herbs.

Unusual Fruit Suspects

Most fruits can no longer be considered exotic. Nearly all are readily available in the larger supermarkets. There are only a few fruits left unrecognised, though we are sure there are many out there yet to be discovered. Here are a few of the less common ones with which to get acquainted.

Guava
Originally from Brazil, the guava comes in a pear or round shape with a yellow-greenish skin. Its pale yellow flesh and edible seeds are delicious in sorbets and purées or in a fresh fruit salad. When preparing the fruit, cut lengthways and scoop out the flesh and seeds.

Kiwi fruit (Chinese gooseberry)
The magic kiwi—ugly on the outside but heaven on the inside—is jam-packed with vitamin C. Its bright green flesh has a tangy sweet flavour. The black seeds are edible too. It makes an attractive garnish and is particularly tasty with strawberries. The kiwi, which is named after the bird as they both have a furry brown skin, has a cousin called the dragon fruit, but it's not as readily available.

Kumquat
Grown in China where it was a symbol of luck and wealth, the kumquat is a close relative of citrus fruits and actually looks like a baby orange. The skin is totally edible and has a sweet, tangy flavour. You can eat them whole or slice them to make a garnish.

Lychee
This fruit is originally from China and was once considered by the Chinese to be a symbol of love. The fresh lychee is rich in

vitamin C, and is round with a ruddy brown peel. The skin is peeled off to reveal a white firm flesh, which is used in exotic fruit salads. There is a stone in the middle, which should be discarded.

Mango

A luscious juicy fruit when ripe, the mango is green and red in colour with a bright orange flesh. It is rich in vitamin C and cleansing to the palate. Serve sliced or puréed. There is a husky nut in the middle, which you must cut around to loosen the fruit. It can be tricky to prepare but it's worth it.

Papaya

A ripe papaya should have a speckled yellow skin. It is also called pawpaw. When you peel off the skin, a fragrant orange sweet flesh is revealed. In the middle of the papaya is a cluster of black seeds, which can be eaten. This fruit is great for your skin, nails and hair.

Passion fruit

Purple and wrinkled on the outside but sweet and golden on the inside. Passion-fruit seeds can be scooped out and served with chocolate mousse and other delights; it is rich in vitamins A and C. Delicious and nutritious.

Physalis

Also known as the Chinese lantern and the Cape gooseberry, this is one of the top restaurants' favourites for crowning desserts. The dull husk should be peeled back to reveal a glossy exotic bright orange orb about the size of a grape. It smells and tastes great. A must for all sweet lovers.

Pomegranate

The pomegranate makes its appearance on our shelves around Halloween. It is a sweet fruit but it is quite difficult to extract the flesh. The fruit is mostly seeds, which are edible; the flesh around them is pink and delicious. The drink grenadine is made from the pomegranate. This fruit has many healing powers and is a favourite with celebrities.

Star fruit

The star fruit is mild and sweet to taste, and when sliced it has a star shape. It is becoming very popular here and makes a quirky garnish. It is yellow in colour and easy to prepare. A must for an exotic fruit salad or to top off a sorbet.

Mangoes

2

starters

thai fish cakes

Serves **4**

Ingredients
1 medium tin of tuna (198g/7oz)
$^1/_2$ teaspoon fresh chopped coriander
1 dessertspoon lemon juice
$^1/_2$ cup breadcrumbs
seasoning—salt and pepper
$^1/_4$ teaspoon Thai red curry paste
1 beaten egg
to coat: 1 cup fine breadcrumbs
to fry: 1 tablespoon vegetable oil
to serve: salad leaves, sweet chilli sauce

Method
Open the tin of tuna and drain away the excess liquid. Place the tuna in a mixing bowl and add the chopped coriander, lemon juice, breadcrumbs, seasoning and red curry paste. Mix together well. Break the egg into a cup and beat with a fork. Add enough to the mixture to make it into a soft texture. Use your hands to roll the mixture into 4 balls, then press the balls down slightly into a patty shape. Place on a plate of fine breadcrumbs and coat the cakes evenly. Chill for $^1/_2$ hour. Add 1 tablespoon of vegetable oil to a frying pan and heat to a medium/low temperature. Fry the fish cakes until golden on both sides. Dab with kitchen paper to remove excess oil, and serve with salad leaves and sweet chilli sauce on the side. Sweet chilli sauce can be bought in most stores.

stuffed mushrooms

Serves **4**

Ingredients
4 large mushrooms
1 cup breadcrumbs
1 teaspoon mixed herbs
1 dessertspoon chopped onion
seasoning—salt and pepper
2 tablespoons melted butter
4 strips bacon or rashers
4 little knobs of butter

Method
Wash and dry mushrooms, cut out the stalk and place the mushrooms on a baking tray, dark side facing up. Put the breadcrumbs in a bowl and mix in the herbs. Chop the onion finely and add to the mixture along with seasoning and melted butter. Mix well. Cut the rashers into strips with a scissors. Using your hands, stuff the mushrooms with the bread mixture and add a little knob of butter on top. Make an X on top of the mushrooms by overlapping 2 strips of bacon. Bake in a moderate oven at 150°C (300°F/gas mark 3) for 15 minutes or until mushrooms are soft. These can be served as a starter or a side dish to accompany any meat or fish.

smoked mackerel pâté with melba toast

Serves **4**

Ingredients
2 smoked mackerel fillets (available vacuum packed usually)
2 tablespoons natural yoghurt
1 tablespoon melted butter
1 dessertspoon lemon juice
black pepper (approx. 4 twists from a peppermill)

Method
Remove the skin from the mackerel and place in a liquidiser with all the other ingredients. Blend until smooth and spoon into a small ramekin or bowl. Place in fridge until ready to eat.

melba toast

Toast 2 slices of white sliced pan and cut off the crusts with a serrated knife. With an adult supervising, slice through the bread horizontally with a sharp knife. Now cut into triangle shapes. Place the now-extra-thin slices under the grill, whiter side up; toast until golden and curled. This takes only a few seconds. Place the pâté on a serving plate and arrange the Melba toast around it. You could also have this for breakfast.

golden fish cakes with cous cous and dill dressing

Serves ❹

Ingredients
200 g (7 oz) cooked white fish (cod or haddock)
slice of lemon
100 g (4 oz) mashed potato
1 teaspoon chopped parsley
1 dessertspoon lemon juice
seasoning—pepper and salt
¹/₂ a beaten egg
4 chives
¹/₂ cup cous cous, soaked in hot water for 20 minutes
to fry: 1 tablespoon vegetable oil
to serve: salad leaves and Dill Dressing (see page 192)

Method
To prepare fish, wash it and place in a pot of cold water with a slice of lemon; let it simmer for 5 minutes. Drain and make sure to remove skin and any bones. Mash with a fork in a bowl, then add the potato, parsley, lemon juice, pepper and salt. Break the egg into a cup and beat with a fork. Add half the beaten egg to the mixture. Chop the chives in with a scissors. Mix well. Shape into 4 balls, using your hands, then flatten slightly to make a patty shape. Drain and squeeze out any excess liquid from the cous cous, then pour it out onto a dinner plate. Toss the fish cakes in the cous cous until they are evenly coated. Chill in the fridge for at least 1 hour. Fry in a warm pan with a little vegetable oil until golden brown. Drain on kitchen paper and serve with salad leaves and dill dressing.

bruschettas

Serves **4**

There are many ways to make this dish but this is our favourite.

Ingredients
1 ciabatta or a thick French bread stick
fresh pesto (see page 62)
4 tomatoes
1 cup grated mozzarella or 4 slices of buffalo mozzerella
$^1/_2$ cup black olives (optional)
1 tablespoon olive oil
to serve: sprig of basil

Method
Cut bread at a slant into slices around $3^1/_2$ cm ($1^1/_2$ in) thick. Place on a baking sheet. Using a pastry brush, paint the top of each piece of bread with olive oil followed by the pesto. Slice the tomatoes finely and place a few slices on top of each piece of bread. Then sprinkle some mozzarella on the tomatoes, and some olive halves if you are using them. Bake in a moderate oven until the cheese melts and the bread is crisp. Serve while still warm, with a sprig of basil for garnish. These are deeeeelicious!

beef koftas

Serves **4**

Ingredients
200 g (7 oz) minced beef
1 tablespoon breadcrumbs
1 clove garlic, crushed
seasoning—salt and pepper
dash of Worcestershire or soy sauce
1 beaten egg
pinch of cardamom powder and a pinch of cumin powder
pinch of ground ginger
to serve: cocktail sticks and an orange and some tin foil (optional)

Method
Mix all the ingredients together in a bowl. Wet hands and shape the mixture into small balls. (By wetting your hands, you prevent the mixture from sticking to them.) Place on a baking tray and bake in a moderate oven for 5 minutes. Remove from the oven, turn them over and rub over with the barbecue sauce. Return to the oven and bake until the juices are clear. Remove from oven and drain on kitchen paper. Rub them over once again with the barbecue sauce (see page 192). Place a cocktail stick in each one. For party display, you could slice the bottom off an orange so that it stands up, then cover the orange with tin foil and stick the koftas into it.

potato cubes with bacon and balsamic dressing

Serves ❹

Ingredients
either 4 medium cooked and peeled potatoes *or* 16 cooked baby potatoes
2 smoked streaky rashers
3 scallions or chives
1 tablespoon vegetable oil
1 clove garlic, crushed
seasoning—salt and pepper
1 dessertspoon balsamic vinegar
coriander or chives for garnish

Method
Cut the potatoes into medium-sized cubes and place in a mixing bowl. Chop the rashers into small strips (using a scissors is easiest). Chop the scallions finely (also using a scissors). Pour the vegetable oil into a small frying pan, heat slightly and add the bacon. Fry until crispy then lower the heat and add the scallions and garlic, stirring them together. Season. Pour in the balsamic vinegar and stand back as it tends to splatter for a second. Stir well then pour over the top of the potatoes. Transfer into a nice serving dish and sprinkle with some chives or coriander. This dish is nicer when served warm.

grilled guacamole nests with prawn & pine nut centre

Serves ❷

Ingredients
1 dessertspoon pine nuts
1 avocado for 2 people
1 teaspoon lemon juice
2 tablespoons cooked prawns
1 dessertspoon mayonnaise
seasoning—pepper and salt
some grated fresh Parmesan cheese

Method
Pop the pine nuts into a dry frying pan and toss on a medium heat until golden. Remove and cool. Cut the avocado into 2 halves; remove and discard the stone. Scoop the flesh out into a bowl and cut into small cubes. Keep the avocado skins for serving. Sprinkle the avocado cubes with lemon juice. Add the pine nuts and prawns and mix well. Stir in the mayonnaise and season. Pile the filling back into the avocado shells and sprinkle with cheese. Place under a hot grill and allow the cheese to brown slightly. Serve with a Caesar salad or alone as a starter.

chicken satay with peanut butter sauce

Serves ❹ as a starter, or ❷ people as a main course, with rice

Ingredients
8 wooden skewers
4 chicken breasts, cut into cubes
seasoning—pepper and salt
2 tablespoons vegetable oil

Sauce
2 tablespoons crunchy peanut butter
1 tablespoon soy sauce
1 dessertspoon brown sugar
1 dessertspoon lemon juice
1 dessertspoon sunflower oil
1 teaspoon Dalkey or other grain mustard
150 ml ($^1/_4$ pint) water

Method
Soak the wooden skewers in cold water for 30 minutes. While you are waiting, wash and pat dry two chicken breasts, then cut them into cubes. Thread the cubes onto the wooden skewers, season and rub with oil. Grill, bake or barbecue them on a medium heat until golden and the chicken is cooked through—this usually takes 10 minutes on each side. Rub over generously with the peanut sauce (see method below). Can be served hot or cold.

Method for sauce
Place all the sauce ingredients in a saucepan and stir gently on a low heat until sauce thickens to medium consistency.

spicy chicken wings

Serves 4

Ingredients
approximately 4 chicken wings per person (These can be bought in packs of 12 in supermarkets)
1 clove garlic, crushed
$^1/_2$ teaspoon ground coriander
$^1/_2$ teaspoon cumin
$^1/_2$ teaspoon cardamom
$^1/_2$ teaspoon garam masala
2 tablespoons vegetable oil

Method
Wash and dry the chicken and cut at the joint in the wings to separate into two pieces. Crush the garlic and mix with the spices and vegetable oil in a bowl. Add in the chicken and stir well until meat is fully coated. Allow to marinate for at least 30 minutes. Place wings on an oiled baking tray and cook in a moderate oven for 15 minutes, then turn over the wings and cook for another 15 minutes or until cooked. When eating, watch out for the bones and make sure you have plenty of paper serviettes available. These are as messy as they are yummy!

fresh salmon pâté

Serves ❹

Ingredients
100 g (4 oz) cooked salmon
slice of lemon
1 dessertspoon lemon juice
1 dessertspoon chopped dill
1 dessertspoon mayonnaise
seasoning—salt and pepper
to decorate: slice of lemon
to serve: Melba toast (see page 40) or plain toast, brown bread or a salad

Method
Poach the fresh salmon—place it in a pot and pour enough boiling water over it to cover it; add a pinch of salt and slice of lemon, and let it simmer for 10 minutes. Remove from the liquid in the pot using a slotted spoon. Place on a plate and allow to cool. Remove the skin and any bones. Place in a food processor or liquidiser with the rest of the ingredients. Process until smooth. Place in a ramekin or bowl and chill until ready to serve. Decorate the top with a twist of lemon. This can be served with Melba or plain toast, brown bread or a salad.

goujons of fresh cod with tartar sauce

Serves ❹

Ingredients
1 fresh medium cod tail, skinned and cut into strips (There are no bones in the tail of cod!)
1 saucer full of flour
1 saucer full of beaten egg
1 saucer full of fine bread crumbs

Tartar sauce
mayonnaise (see below)
a few capers (to taste)
a squeeze of lemon
chopped parsley

Method
Cut the cod into strips, lengthways about 6 cm ($2^1/_2$ in) long. Dip the strips of fish in the flour then the beaten egg, and finally cover evenly with the breadcrumbs. Deep fry until golden brown. Drain on kitchen paper and then serve immediately.

Tartar sauce is simply mayonnaise with a few capers (to taste) and a squeeze of lemon and chopped parsley mixed well into it.

mayonnaise

Ingredients
1 egg
1 dessertspoon white wine vinegar
$1^1/_2$ cups vegetable oil (approximately)
seasoning—salt and pepper
$^1/_4$ teaspoon Dijon mustard

Break the egg into the liquidiser, add the vinegar and blend for a few seconds. Turn on again and add the oil very slowly through the hole in the top of the liquidiser lid until the mayonnaise has reached required thickness (you may not need the full amount of oil, so keep an eye on the consistency and stop adding when it is correct). Add some seasoning and mustard. To finish off into tartar sauce, add the capers and lemon juice. Refrigerate the excess.

potato cakes

Serves **4**

Ingredients
200 g (8 oz) mashed potato
50 g (2 oz) white flour
seasoning—pepper and salt
a pinch of mixed herbs (optional)
50 g (2 oz) melted butter
to fry: **25 g (1 oz) butter and 1 dessertspoon vegetable oil**
to serve: **a little grated cheese (optional)**

Method
Place the potato in a mixing bowl. Add the flour and seasoning, herbs and melted butter, and mix well. Using your hands, form the mixture into one big ball. Sprinkle some flour out on a plastic board or other flat surface and press out the ball of mixture into a flat circle, like a pizza. Now cut out as you would a pizza into 8 wedges. Melt the butter and oil in a frying pan. When it is simmering, add the potato cakes and fry until golden. Turn over and fry the other side until golden also. Drain off the excess oil by removing the potato cakes from the pan and placing them on some kitchen paper. Serve with a sprinkle of grated cheese on top for an extra tasty treat.

pasta salad with char-grilled chicken, honey & mustard dressing or pesto

Serves ❹

Ingredients
2 cups of penne pasta
2 chicken breasts
salad leaves

Dressing
1 dessertspoon white wine vinegar
3 dessertspoons olive oil
1 teaspoon honey
1 teaspoon grain mustard
seasoning—pepper & salt

Method
Put the pasta in a pot of boiling lightly salted water and cook for 10 minutes or until *aldente* (For full instructions, see page 25). When it's cooked, drain and place in a bowl of cold water, and set aside. You can barbecue, grill or boil the chicken (boil by placing in a saucepan of boiling water for 15 minutes). Boiling is a better option as grilling can take a long time to cook the chicken all the way through.

Method for honey and mustard dressing
Put all the ingredients in a screw-top jar and shake.

Cool the chicken and cut into slices. Drain the pasta and place in a bowl on top of salad leaves. Add the chicken and dressing or the pesto. Season. To make pesto, see Pasta Pesto dish (p.62).

Alternatively, place the cooked pasta in a bowl, add sliced chicken and dressing and mix well. When serving, arrange some green salad leaves on 4 serving plates and top with pasta and chicken, then drizzle with dressing.

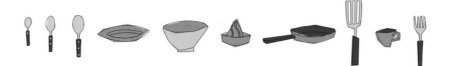

crab cakes

Serves **4** as a starter, or can be used as a main course with two cakes per person

Ingredients
100 g (4 oz) white crab meat (available in vacuum packs in most supermarkets or from your local fish shop)
3 tablespoons breadcrumbs
1 teaspoon chopped dill
1 dessertspoon lime juice
1 dessertspoon chopped coriander
$^1/_2$ beaten egg
seasoning—salt and pepper
to coat: a dinner plate full of breadcrumbs
to fry: a tablespoon of vegetable oil
to serve: mixed leaves of lettuce and sweet chilli sauce

Method
In a bowl, combine all of the ingredients (except those for coating and frying) and mix together well. Using your hands, roll the mixture into four balls, then press each out into a burger shape, and roll in the breadcrumbs until coated. Chill in the refrigerator for 30 minutes. Heat the oil in a frying pan, preferably a non-stick pan. Place the chilled crab cakes on the pan and fry until golden brown on each side. Remove from the pan and place on kitchen paper to drain any excess oil. Serve with mixed leaves of lettuce and sweet chilli sauce.

aubergine pâté

Serves **4**

Ingredients
1 medium aubergine
1 tablespoon olive oil
seasoning—salt and pepper
2 tablespoons lemon juice
1 clove garlic, crushed
1 teaspoon chopped parsley
1 tablespoon chopped basil
1 slice white bread

Method
Cut the aubergine in two, and place on a baking tray. Rub each half with olive oil and sprinkle with salt and pepper. Place in the oven at 160°C (350°F/gas mark 4) and bake for 10 minutes. Remove from the oven and scoop the flesh from the inside of the aubergine into a bowl—the flesh should be quite soft at this stage. Discard the skins. Add the rest of the ingredients to the bowl, and mix well. Pour the mixture into the food processor. Tear up the bread and add it to the mixture. Blend until smooth. Place in a ramekin dish and serve warm or cold with Melba toast (see page 40).

prawn cocktail

Serves **4**

Ingredients
200 g (8 oz) frozen cooked prawns (defrosted)
2 cups shredded butterhead or iceberg lettuce

Sauce
1 cup mayonnaise
1 tablespoon tomato ketchup
dash of Tabasco (optional)
to serve: 4 twists of lemon, 4 cherry tomatoes and some cocktail sticks (optional)

Method
For four people, you will need four nice decorative dishes or glasses. Wash and dry the lettuce, then shred it thinly with a knife. Place the lettuce in the base of the glasses. In a separate bowl, mix the mayonnaise with the tomato ketchup and the Tabasco. You can add a little more tomato ketchup to get a deeper pink colour if you wish. Squeeze out all the excess water from the prawns; add to the bowl with the mayonnaise mix. Stir together well. Spoon onto the lettuce in each glass and decorate with a twist of lemon. Alternatively, using cocktail sticks, called swizzle sticks, thread a couple of prawns on each, then a cherry tomato, then a couple more prawns, and finish with a twist of lemon. Stand up in the glasses containing the lettuce. This is a great old favourite and the presentation can make it fun too!

crunchy garlic mussels

Serves **4**

Ingredients
12 medium to large mussels
1 clove garlic
1 tablespoon chopped onion
cold water

Topping
75 g (3 oz) butter
2 cloves garlic, crushed
1 dessertspoon chopped parsley
1 tablespoon fine breadcrumbs
to finish: **a dinner plate of fine bread-**
crumbs
to serve: **wedges of lemon, and finger**
bowls

Method
Scrub the mussels under running water, removing any barnacles and beard. Discard any mussels that are open and do not close when tapped with a finger. Place the mussels in a saucepan with enough cold water to cover the base of the pot. Chop the clove of garlic into four pieces and add it to the pot along with the onion. Place on the cooker, cover with a lid and bring to the boil. Turn down the heat and allow to simmer for five minutes, or until all of the mussels have opened. Remove from the heat and strain off the liquid. Discard the onion and garlic. Allow the mussels to cool and then remove the empty shell and discard. **Never use a mussel that does not open after cooking.** Discard.

Method for topping
To make the topping, cream the butter, garlic, parsley and fine breadcrumbs together. For tips for making breadcrumbs, see page 13.

Using a knife, spread the topping mixture over the top of each mussel, making sure that the shell is filled up. Smooth over the top and then press the buttered mussel down onto the plate of finely chopped breadcrumbs and coat the entire surface area well. Place on a baking tray and put into a hot oven for 5 minutes or under the grill to brown the tops. Serve on a plate, with mussels fanned out and a wedge of lemon. It is best to serve these with a finger bowl as they are messy!

melon cocktail

Serves ❹

There are many types of melon available—our favourite for this recipe is the galia, but feel free to experiment.

Ingredients
1 melon
slice of lemon
2 tablespoons castor sugar
1-2 drops food colouring (cochineal or green is best)
4 teaspoons orange or blackcurrant cordial
to garnish: 4 sprigs of mint

Method
You will need four stemmed glasses for presentation. Rub the rims of the glasses over with lemon juice. Place the sugar and food colouring on a plate so that the colouring is blended through the sugar. Dip the rim of each glass in the coloured sugar. Pour a teaspoon of cordial into the bottom of each glass. Using a melon baller or a teaspoon, scoop out the melon in balls and fill up each glass. Decorate with a sprig of mint. Keep chilled until ready to serve. Simple.

deep-fried camembert with red onion marmalade

Serves ❹

Ingredients
1 box of Camembert (choose the type that has 4 or 6 individual triangles in it)
1 beaten egg
a plateful of fine breadcrumbs
Red Onion Marmalade
1 tablespoon vegetable oil
1 small red onion, finely chopped
1 teaspoon garlic (creamed or crushed)
1 teaspoon brown sugar
1 dessertspoon red wine vinegar

Method
Dip the triangles of cheese in the beaten egg, then coat well with the breadcrumbs. Place on a plate and chill for 30 minutes in the fridge or a cold room. Heat the deep fat fryer to 190°C (375°F). Lower the coated cheese pieces into the hot fat and cook for 4 to 5 minutes until golden and crisp. Remove and place on kitchen paper to drain. Serve with the marmalade as set out below, or with a nice coulis.

Method for red onion marmalade
Heat the oil in a small saucepan. Add the chopped onion and sauté for 5 minutes. Now add the garlic and sugar, stirring it in well. Add the vinegar, then cover the saucepan and allow the mixture to simmer on low heat for approximately 7 to 8 minutes or until the onion is soft. This can be served either hot or cold to accompany many dishes. It can be stored in the fridge in a jar for 3 to 4 days.

smoked salmon coronets with avocado salsa

Serves ❹

Ingredients
1 ripe avocado
4 vine cherry tomatoes (cut in quarters)
1 small red onion (chopped finely)
3 tablespoons olive oil
juice of 1 lime (or lemon)
1 dessertspoon chopped dill
1 teaspoon Dalkey or any grain mustard
1 teaspoon honey (runny type)
seasoning—pepper and salt
200 g (8 oz) sliced smoked salmon

Method
To prepare the salsa, cut the avocado in half lengthways and remove stone. Using a dessertspoon, carefully remove the flesh of the avocado and chop roughly into a bowl. Add all of the rest of the ingredients, except the salmon. Mix together well. Lay a slice of the smoked salmon out flat and spoon some of the salsa in and roll up into a cone shape. Serve on individual plates and drizzle more of the salsa around each serving. This tastes heavenly.

Brusche

Bruschettas

Potato cubes with bacon & balsamic dressing

Pasta pesto

Deep-fried camembert with red onion marmalade

Bruschetta

Grilled guacamole nests with prawn and pine nut centre

vol au-vents with chicken and mushroom in a creamy tarragon sauce

Serves ❹

Ingredients

4 frozen medium-sized vol-au-vent cases
a little egg wash (optional)
1 tablespoon vegetable oil
8 medium mushrooms
1 clove garlic, crushed
2 cooked chicken breasts cut into small cubes*
seasoning—pepper and salt

Sauce
25 g (1 oz) butter
25 g (1 oz) white flour
125 ml (4¹/₂ fl oz) cream
2 tablespoons water
1 dessertspoon chopped tarragon
to finish: Parmesan cheese, grated (optional)

Method

*To cook the chicken breasts: clean them and place them in a saucepan with enough cold water to cover them. Add a sprig of tarragon or thyme. Bring to the boil, then turn down to simmer for 15 minutes. Drain and allow to cool, then cut into small dice sizes. The leftover juices from cooking the chicken breasts can be used instead of the water in the making of the sauce, if you wish.

Rub over the top of the frozen vol-au-vent cases with a little egg wash if you like. Place on a wetted baking tray and bake in a hot oven (200°C/400°F/gas mark 8) for 5 minutes. Reduce the heat to 180°C (350°F/gas mark 6) and bake until golden for approximately 10 more minutes. Remove to cool on a wire tray. Using a teaspoon, remove the centre piece of pastry and set aside to use later.

For the filling, heat the oil in a frying pan and sauté the mushrooms and garlic for a few minutes until soft. Place in a bowl with the chopped chicken, seasoning and chopped tarragon.

Method for creamy tarragon sauce

Melt the butter in a small saucepan, then add the flour. Blend them together and allow to cook for a few minutes. Remove from the heat! Combine the cream and water together and add to the pot slowly, stirring all the time. Once blended with the roux (flour and butter paste), return the pot to the heat. Stir all the time and return to the boil, then turn down to simmer. If the mixture looks too thick, add a little more water to thin it out. Add the chicken and mushroom mixture and simmer for 5 minutes. Spoon the mixture into the vol-au-vent cases, pop the little pastry lid on top and then place on a baking tray and return to the oven until very hot. You may sprinkle with a little grated Parmesan cheese, if you wish.

buttons and bows

Serves ❹

Ingredients
4 cups of cooked pasta bows/farfalle (2 cups uncooked pasta will make 4 cups cooked pasta)
75 g (3 oz) button mushrooms
2 tablespoons olive oil
1 clove garlic, crushed
50 g (2 oz) cherry tomatoes
8 torn basil leaves
seasoning—pepper and salt
to finish: Parmesan cheese, grated

Method

Place the hot cooked pasta in a bowl. For method for cooking and reheating pasta, see page 25. Wash the mushrooms and drain off on a little kitchen paper. In a frying pan, heat the olive oil, add the whole button mushrooms and fry, stirring gently, for a few minutes. Add the garlic and sauté for one further minute. Add the cherry tomatoes, and cook for one more minute, then remove pan from the heat. Add the contents of the pan to the pasta in the bowl. Add the torn basil leaves and seasoning, and mix well. Serve in individual serving dishes and sprinkle with Parmesan cheese. Add more olive oil if needed. Serve while still hot.

pasta pesto

Serves **4**

Ingredients
2 cups uncooked pasta
pinch of salt

Pesto
1 cup fresh basil leaves
1 dessertspoon pine nuts
1 dessertspoon freshly grated Parmesan cheese
1 clove garlic, crushed
¹/₂ cup olive oil
to serve: grated Parmesan cheese

Method
Place all the pesto ingredients in a food processor and switch on for 1 minute until everything is chopped well into a smooth paste. The amount of olive oil depends on whether you are going to use the pesto for dips or fillings. For dips, the amount above is fine. However, if, as with this recipe, you want to put it with pasta, add a little more oil to spread it further.

Put the uncooked pasta into a pot of boiling lightly salted water. Boil until *aldente* (that means until the pasta is soft but not mushy, firm but not hard). Drain in a colander and run the cold tap through it to wash off excess starch.

If you are making pasta ahead of time, it can be preserved in a container of cold water and drained out when ready to use. Reheat using the microwave or by pouring hot water over it. Once the pasta has been reheated, add the pesto and mix well. Serve with extra parmesan cheese sprinkled over the top.

avocado sailboats with mango salsa

Serves ❹

Ingredients
2 avocados
1 tablespoon lemon juice
2 sticks of celery

Salsa
1 mango or a cup of tinned mango
1 small red chilli
¹/₄ teaspoon creamed garlic

1 dessertspoon chopped red onion
2 dessertspoons lime juice
4 cherry tomatoes, cut into quarters
3 dessertspoons olive oil
1 dessertspoon chopped coriander

to serve
four sticks celery with the leaves attached
additional chopped coriander

Method
Cut avocados in two. Remove stones and rub the avocado with lemon juice. Cover and leave aside.

Method for salsa
If using fresh mango, cut close to the stone, cutting away as much fruit as you can. Peel away the skin from the flesh and cut the flesh into cubes. Cut the chilli in two and scrape out the seeds. Chop into tiny pieces. Wash your hands with cold water to remove all the chilli. Cream the garlic (see page 19). Halve a red onion and chop it finely. Place the mango in a bowl and add the rest of the ingredients. Mix well.

To serve:
Sit the avocado halves in a dish and fill each cavity with salsa mixture. In each avocado half, arrange a stick of celery, with the leaves attached—it should stick upright to resemble a sail boat. Sprinkle with chopped coriander.

Chorizo & white bean soup

AND U2//HOW TO DISMANTLE AN ATOMI

3

mains

chicken coconut curry with noodles

Serves **4**

Ingredients
4 chicken breasts
1 small onion
50 g (2 oz) mushrooms
1 tablespoon vegetable oil
2 cloves garlic
1 teaspoon hot curry powder
1 tablespoon plain white flour
200 ml (7 fl oz) chicken stock
200 ml (7 fl oz) cream
1 tablespoon creamed coconut or 2 tablespoons coconut milk
seasoning—salt and pepper
2 packet egg noodles

Method
Clean then cut the chicken breasts into cubes and set aside. Dice the onion into small pieces. Wash and dry the mushrooms and cut each one into three pieces. Heat the oil in a saucepan and sauté the onion and mushroom for a few minutes—do not cook until brown, just till soft and opaque. Cream the garlic (see page 19) and add it to the pan, stirring for a few seconds. Then add the curry powder and the flour. Stir quickly into the mixture; then remove from the hob to a cool surface. When the mixture is no longer sizzling, pour in the chicken stock and the cream. Stir well and return to the hob, turning up the heat. (Removing the mixture from the heat to add the fluid is what prevents the mixture from going lumpy!) Now add the coconut and the diced chicken, stirring all the time until it comes to the boil. Once it has boiled, turn the heat down low and leave to simmer for 20 minutes or so. Season—add salt and pepper—until you are satisfied with the taste. Boil the noodles according to the instructions on the packet. Drain the noodles. (If you prepare the noodles ahead of time, leave them standing in a pot of cold water, and reheat them in the microwave before serving. This prevents them from getting sticky.) Serve by making a nest of noodles and spooning the curry mixture into the middle. Yummy!

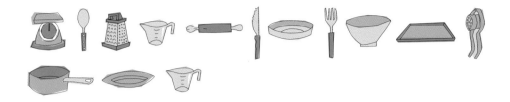

roasted red onion broccoli tart with blue balsamic sauce

Serves ❹

Ingredients
100 g (4 oz) plain flour
pinch of salt
50 g (2 oz) hard margarine
cold water

Filling
125 ml (4¹/₂ fl oz) milk
2 eggs (medium)

seasoning—salt and pepper
1 medium-sized red onion
2 cloves garlic, crushed
1 tablespoon olive oil
100 g (4 oz) broccoli florets
25 g (1 oz) white cheddar cheese, grated
to serve: blue balsamic sauce (see page 191)

Method
Place flour and salt in a bowl, cut the margarine into cubes and rub into the flour with the tips of your fingers until mixture looks like fine bread crumbs. Add just enough cold water (trickle in slowly, dribble by dribble) to mix to a soft dough, using your hands. Turn onto a floured work surface or board and knead lightly. Roll out with a rolling pin to fit an 18 cm (7 in) round tin. Press carefully into the well-greased tin and trim the excess pastry off around the edges with a butter knife. Place pastry in fridge while preparing the filling. Always keep pastry as cool as possible!

Method for filling
Pour the milk into a jug and add 2 medium eggs. Beat well with a fork or whisk. Add a pinch of salt and pepper to season. Peel and slice the red onion and place in a baking tray. Rub over with the crushed garlic, sprinkle with olive oil and bake in the oven at 160°C (350°F/gas mark 4) for 5 minutes. Place on top of chilled pastry. Put the broccoli in a pot of boiling water and boil for 5 minutes. Drain the broccoli well (shake it out to remove excess water) and place on the pastry. Pour in the egg and milk mixture and sprinkle with grated cheese. Bake at 160°C (350°F/gas mark 4–5) for 40 minutes or until set and golden brown. Lift or slide out of the tin onto a plate. Cut into slices and serve with blue balsamic sauce (see page 191).

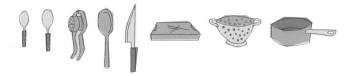

prawn provençale with rice

Serves ❹

Ingredients

1 medium onion
1 clove garlic (creamed or crushed)
1 tablespoon olive oil
1 tin chopped tomatoes
1 dessertspoon tomato purée
1 handful fresh chopped basil
seasoning—salt and pepper
200 g (8 oz) fresh or frozen and thawed prawns
2 cups long-grain rice
to serve: a sprig of basil

> **Tips on Rice**
> Every cup of raw (uncooked) rice yields 2 cups of cooked rice. To every cup of uncooked rice add 2 cups of cold water and bring to the boil.

Method

Chop the onion into small pieces and crush the garlic or cream it using the method outlined on page 19. Heat the olive oil in a pan and sauté the onions and garlic for a few minutes. Add the can of tomatoes, the tomato purée, the basil and a pinch of salt and pepper. Simmer for 5 minutes (simmering is cooking on a low to medium heat where the mixture will bubble very little). Add the prawns and continue to simmer for 10 minutes until the prawns are cooked. If using frozen prawns, defrost first and add to sauce for 5 minutes. Serve on a bed of rice (see below) with a sprig of basil on top.

To cook rice

Place the rice in a saucepan with 4 cups of water and heat to the boil. Once it comes to the boil, lower the heat and simmer for 10 minutes or until *al dente* (this means until soft but not mushy, firm but not hard). Drain in a colander or sieve and run some hot water over the rice to wash off extra starch. Shake well and leave to drain for a little while in colander or sieve until all the water is gone. Spoon onto plate. Rice can also be prepared ahead of time and preserved cold, then drained and very effectively reheated in the microwave.

stir-fried prawns

Serves ❹

Ingredients

1 packet egg noodles or French bread to accompany
2 scallions
1 tablespoon olive oil
1 clove garlic (creamed or crushed—for tips on creaming garlic, see page 19)
1 teaspoon chopped ginger
200g (8 oz) frozen prawns or prawn tails
1 teaspoon brown sugar
juice of one lime
a dash of fish sauce
1 teaspoon soy sauce
1 cup bean sprouts
to decorate: **some sliced carrot**

Method

Follow the instructions on the packet for preparing the noodles, if using. Have them ready to serve with the stir-fry as soon as it is ready.

Cook the stir-fry immediately prior to serving. It is one dish for which it is recommended that you prepare all of the ingredients before beginning to cook. Slice the scallions into small discs, making sure to use the green stalk also. Heat the oil to a medium heat in a wok or frying pan and add the scallions. Add in the garlic and pop in the chopped ginger. Stir fry for 1 minute. Now add the prawns and stir. You can add extra sliced vegetables if desired, such as mangetout, baby corn or mushrooms. Sprinkle in the sugar, lime juice, fish sauce and soy sauce, and stir fry for 3 minutes. Add the bean sprouts and stir for 1 minute. Serve mixture on a bed of egg noodles or with French bread. Decorate with some sliced carrot, if desired.

pasta with herbs, garlic and olive oil

Serves **4**

Ingredients
2 cups uncooked short-cut pasta
2 tablespoons olive oil
1 clove garlic (crushed or creamed)
1 handful chopped fresh basil & parsley
$^1/_2$ teaspoon thyme
$^1/_2$ teaspoon oregano
$^1/_2$ teaspoon marjoram
freshly milled or ground black pepper
5 cherry tomatoes
to serve: **Parmesan cheese, freshly grated**

Method
Cook pasta by adding it to a pot of boiling, lightly salted water. Cook until *al dente* (that means until the pasta is soft but not mushy, firm but not hard). Drain in a colander and run the cold tap through it to wash off excess starch. If you are making pasta ahead of time, it can be preserved in a container of cold water and drained when ready to use. Reheat using the microwave or by pouring hot water over it. In a saucepan, heat the oil, then add the garlic and all the herbs. Sauté lightly for a minute or two until garlic is cooked. Pour over drained pasta. Slice the cherry tomatoes in half and stir them in. Sprinkle with freshly grated Parmesan cheese and serve. Add more olive oil if desired.

bee's pizza pie

Serves ❹

Ingredients

Base
1 dessertspoon dried yeast
125 ml (4 fl oz) lukewarm water
1 teaspoon sugar
200 g (8 oz) strong flour
a pinch of salt
1 dessertspoon vegetable oil

Topping
1 onion
1 clove garlic, crushed
1 tablespoon olive oil
1 tin chopped tomatoes
1 teaspoon Italian seasoning/oregano
salt and pepper
100 g (4 oz) mozzarella cheese, grated
12 slices pepperoni

Method for base

Dissolve the dried yeast in the lukewarm water with 1 teaspoon of sugar. Sieve the flour and salt into a bowl and warm it up by putting it in the oven or microwave until it is warm to the touch. Add the yeasty water to the warm flour and pour in the vegetable oil. Beat well. Cover the bowl with a clean tea towel and put aside in a warm place to rise for 30 minutes. When it has risen, knead and roll it out to fit the pizza tin. (If you are using instant dried yeast, follow instructions on packet.)

Method for topping

Dice the onion into small pieces and crush the garlic. Heat the oil in the saucepan, pop in the onions and garlic, and sauté for a few minutes. Add the chopped tomatoes and Italian seasoning, and season with salt and pepper. Cook for a few minutes. Spread this mixture on the base, and sprinkle the grated cheese over it. Arrange the pepperoni around the top. You can, of course, use any other pizza topping you wish, such as mushrooms, peppers, cooked sausage or chicken—use your imagination! Bake in a moderate oven (140°–160°C/275°–315°F/gas mark 5–6) for 35 minutes or until the base is cooked. Cut into slices and enjoy.

lamb shish kebabs with raita and spicy cous cous

Serves ❹

Ingredients
Shish kebabs
4 wooden skewers
200 g (8 oz) minced lamb
2 tablespoons bread crumbs
1 clove garlic, crushed
1 teaspoon grated ginger
1 teaspoon cumin powder
1 beaten egg
a dash of Worcestershire sauce
seasoning

Raita
1 cup grated cucumber
$^1/_2$ teaspoon crushed garlic
$^1/_2$ cup natural yoghurt
1 dessertspoon chopped mint
$^1/_2$ teaspoon cumin powder

Method
Soak the wooden skewers in cold water to prevent them from burning. Mix all the shish kebab ingredients together in a bowl. Shape into 4 sausage shapes with your hands and put a wooden skewer lengthways through each one. Place them on a greased baking tray and bake in a moderate oven (140°–160°C/275°–315°F/gas mark 4–5) for 20 minutes, turning over once after the first 10 minutes.

Method for raita
Place all the raita ingredients together in a bowl and mix well.
Place each shish kebab on a plate with a portion of spicy cous cous (and a small bowl of raita.)

spicy cous cous

Ingredients
1 cup cous cous
1 cup boiling water
1 tablespoon vegetable oil
$^1/_2$ teaspoon garlic, crushed
$^1/_2$ teaspoon cumin powder
$^1/_2$ teaspoon dried coriander
$^1/_2$ teaspoon chilli powder
to season: **pepper and salt**

Method
Place cous cous in a bowl. Add boiling water and leave to soak for 5 minutes.

In the meantime, put oil in a small frying pan. Add garlic and all the spices. Simmer for a few minutes on a moderate heat. Pour over soaked cous cous and mix well. Add pepper and salt to taste.

chilli nachos

Serves ❹

Ingredients

Chilli

1 medium onion
1 teaspoon olive oil
1 clove garlic, crushed
500 g (1 lb) minced beef
1 tin chopped tomatoes
dash of Tabasco sauce
2 teaspoons tomato purée
$^1/_2$ teaspoon chilli powder
1 teaspoon vinegar
1 teaspoon sugar
about $^1/_4$ cup water

Guacamole

1 ripe avocado
$^1/_2$ clove garlic, crushed
juice of $^1/_2$ lime

1 large bag tortilla chips
grated cheese of your choice
sour cream
2 chopped cherry tomatoes

Method

To make the chilli, finely chop the onion, put the olive oil in a frying pan and fry with the crushed garlic for a few seconds. Then add the minced beef and cook until browned. Now add all of the rest of the chilli ingredients. Bring to the boil. Once boiled, turn down and simmer for 8 to 10 minutes. Set aside.

Method for guacamole

Slice the avocado in two. Remove the stone and discard. Spoon out the flesh, then mash well with a fork. Add the garlic and lime juice. Mix well.

Put the tortilla chips on a baking tray and sprinkle with lots of grated cheese. Place under the grill until cheese has melted, then transfer onto a large plate. Place chilli beef mixture in a bowl and garnish with the chopped cherry tomatoes. Serve the guacamole and sour cream in small bowls. For a TV feast, pour the chilli on top of the chips and drizzle the guacamole and sour cream on top.

crispy chicken with a garlic centre

Serves ❹

Ingredients
75 g (3 oz) butter
2 cloves garlic (crushed or creamed)
pepper
1 teaspoon chopped parsley
4 chicken breasts
for coating: 1 beaten egg on a plate, a plate of flour and a plate of fine bread crumbs

Method
Put the butter, garlic, pepper and chopped parsley in a bowl and mash together with a fork. (For tips on creaming garlic, see page 19.) Make into a sausage shape and wrap in cling film, then chill in the fridge or freezer until solid. Wash the chicken breasts, then make a slit down the side of each. Remove the garlic butter from freezer, cut into four and insert a piece into each of the chicken breasts. Press the slit closed.

To coat the chicken, first beat the egg and pour out onto a dinner plate, then pour a dinner plate of flour and a dinner plate of breadcrumbs. (For tips on breadcrumbs, see page 13.) Dip the chicken breasts in the flour, then dip them into the beaten egg, and finally coat them well with the breadcrumbs. Lay them onto another plate and chill them in the fridge for 15 minutes or so. Deep fry until golden brown on the outside. Drain them off on tissue paper and then place them on a baking tray and bake in the oven at 150°C (315°F/gas mark 4) for 15 minutes. If a deep fat fryer is not available, heat a little olive oil in a frying pan and fry each breast until golden on each side, then finish in oven as with other method. These are delicious served with a Caesar salad.

oriental pork with noodles

Serves **4**

Ingredients

2 tablespoons cornflour
400 g (14 oz) pork pieces (can be purchased pre-cut)
1 tablespoon vegetable oil
1 medium onion
3 bell peppers (1 red, 1 yellow and 1 green)
1 clove garlic (creamed or crushed)
1 cup chicken stock or water
$^1/_2$ cup cider or apple juice
1 teaspoon fennel seeds (wrapped in muslin)
seasoning—salt and pepper
Chinese noodles

Method

Put the cornflour on a dinner plate and coat the pork pieces in it. Warm a little oil in a saucepan and fry the pork until golden brown. Remove pork and place on a plate. Chop the onion and peppers and add to the same pot you have been using. Add another drop of oil if necessary. Fry for 1 minute then add crushed garlic and stir. (For tips on creaming garlic, see page 19.) Now pour in the stock and the cider (or apple juice). Add the fennel seeds wrapped in the muslin. Bring to the boil and pop in the pork. Stir well and season. Reduce the heat and let simmer with the lid on the saucepan until the pork is tender (around 30 minutes). Before serving, remove the muslin bag containing fennel seeds. Serve with Chinese noodles prepared according to the instructions on the packet.

fillet steak wrap with sour cream and chive dip

Serves ❹

Ingredients
200 g (8 oz) fillet steak cut into thin slices
1 medium onion
1 tablespoon olive oil
4 wraps or soft taco tortillas
10 chives
1 cup sour cream
salt and pepper
to serve: **¹/₂ head of lettuce (optional)**

Method
Slice the steak into long, thin strips. Slice the onion into very fine rings. Heat the oil in frying pan until fairly hot. Season and fry each slice of steak on a medium heat, until beige in colour, turning while cooking. Be careful not to overcook as steak cooks quickly. Remove from heat and drain on some kitchen paper. Add the onion and another drop of oil, then fry the onion slices until golden. Wash the pan and put it back on a medium heat. Place the tortillas in the pan for 30 seconds each side. Remove to plates. Place the steak and onion on one side of the tortilla wrap and fold in half. Using a scissors, cut the chives into tiny pieces in a bowl, and blend together with the sour cream. Serve the wraps with a blob of the sour cream dip and finely sliced lettuce, if using.

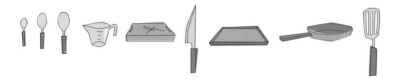

chicken paprika

Serves **4**

Ingredients
4 chicken breasts
2 dessertspoons paprika
3 dessertspoons flour
2 tablespoons olive oil
1 small onion
1 teaspoon oil, for frying onion
200 ml (7 fl oz) chicken stock
100 ml (4 fl oz) cream or a small carton of natural yoghurt
1 teaspoon tomato purée
salt and pepper

Method
Clean the chicken breasts and pat dry. Coat with paprika by placing the paprika and the flour in a plastic bag with the chicken—hold the bag tightly closed and shake until the chicken is well coated. Heat the oil in a frying pan and gently fry the chicken for about 5 minutes on each side. Remove from the pan and place on a baking tray in the oven at 120°C (250°F/gas mark 1) to keep it hot. Chop the onion finely then sauté in a pan with a little oil. Now add the stock and the cream or yoghurt. Add the tomato purée. Bring to the boil, stirring occasionally. Once it has boiled, turn down to simmer until the mixture has thickened slightly, then season with salt and pepper until you are satisfied with the taste. Serve this sauce poured over the chicken with rice, potatoes or salad as an accompaniment.

fettuccini with creamy garlic and bacon sauce

Serves ❹

Ingredients
allow 25g (1 oz) of uncooked pasta per person
4 smoked streaky rashers
1 tablespoon olive oil
1 clove garlic
25 g (1 oz) butter
25 g (1 oz) white flour
125 ml (4¹/₂ fl oz) cream
125 ml (4¹/₂ fl oz) chicken stock or water
pepper and salt
to serve: grated Parmesan cheese and black pepper, if desired

Method
Cook pasta in lightly salted water until *aldente* (this means soft but not mushy, firm but not hard). Drain and keep in a bowl of cold water until needed. (See page 25 for more on cooking pasta.)

To make the sauce, first chop the rashers with a scissors into small pieces, then heat the oil in a small pan and fry the chopped rashers until crispy. Cream or crush the garlic (see page 19) and add to the bacon. Stir on a low heat for about 1 minute. Remove to a plate and wash and dry the pan before making the sauce. Place the butter in the pan and allow to melt over a low heat, add the flour and mix well until paste-like. Remove pan from the heat. When it has stopped sizzling, add half of the cream and half of the stock/water and stir well. Return to the heat and turn it up. Now allow the sauce to come to a good simmer, stirring all the time until it has thickened. Add the rest of the cream and stock/water, little by little, until the sauce has reached the desired thickness (not runny but not too heavy or gummy). Simmer for another 5–10 minutes, then add the cooked bacon and garlic. Season. Remember to check the flavour as you add salt and pepper.

Drain the pasta and reheat in the microwave or by pouring hot water over it. Combine the pasta and the sauce. Serve in a nice dish or bowl, sprinkled with freshly grated Parmesan cheese and a little black pepper if desired.

sweet pepper penne

Serves ❹

Ingredients
2 cups uncooked penne pasta
1 large pointed sweet red bell pepper
3 spring onions
¹/₂ clove crushed garlic
2 dessertspoons olive oil
3 chopped fresh tomatoes
1 teaspoon fennel seeds
3 dessertspoons balsamic vinegar
¹/₂ teaspoon sugar
seasoning—salt and pepper
to serve: freshly chopped basil, freshly grated Parmesan cheese, black cracked pepper

Method
Cook pasta in lightly salted water for 12 minutes or until *aldente* (this means soft but not mushy, firm but not hard). Drain and keep in a bowl of cold water until needed. (For more tips on cooking pasta, see page 25.)

Slice the pepper into rings, making sure to remove seeds and pith from inside. Chop the spring onions finely. Heat the olive oil in a saucepan, then fry the spring onions, pepper slices and crushed garlic for a few minutes. Chop up the fresh tomatoes and add them to the pan, followed by the fennel seeds, vinegar and sugar. Simmer until peppers are soft and tender. Season with salt and pepper and place on top of drained pasta. Sprinkle with basil and some freshly grated Parmesan cheese and black cracked pepper.

This dish is seasonal as the pointed peppers are available only at certain times of the year.

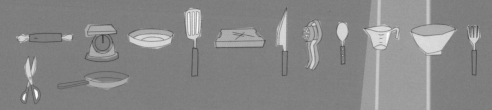

smoky bacon and goat's cheese tartlets

Serves **4**

Ingredients
Pastry
150 g (6 oz) plain flour
pinch of salt
75 g (3 oz) hard margarine
cold water
Filling
125 ml (4¹/₂ fl oz) milk
2 medium eggs

seasoning—a pinch of salt and
pepper
1 chopped onion
4 smoked skinless streaky rashers
1 tablespoon olive oil
1 clove garlic, crushed
100 g (4 oz) goat's cheese
4 cherry tomatoes

Method
You will need 4 tartlet tins, each measuring 10 cm (4 in) in diameter, or 1 tin measuring 20 cm (8 in) in diameter. Grease well and set aside.

To make the pastry, place the flour in a bowl, add a pinch of salt and the hard margarine, cut up into small cubes. Rub the margarine into the flour using your fingertips until mixture looks like fine breadcrumbs and there are no lumps left. Add cold water, dribble by dribble, using enough to form the mixture into a soft dough—it should be neither crumbly nor wet to the touch. Form into a ball and lay out on a flat surface that has been lightly dusted with flour. Knead lightly by balling the pastry and repeatedly turning it back in towards itself. Roll the pastry out flat and from it cut four circles to fit down into the four tins (or one, if you're using a large tin). Press the dough into the tin and use a knife to trim off any excess dough. Place the tin(s) on a baking tray and chill in the fridge or other cool place until needed.

Method for filling
Measure the milk into a jug. Add the eggs and beat well. Add seasoning. Chop the onion and bacon finely (the bacon is easier to cut if you use a scissors!) Heat the oil in a frying pan, add the onion and bacon and fry for a few minutes. Add crushed garlic. (See page 19 for tips on garlic.) Scoop the mixture over the top of the pastry in the tartlet tins. Add a slice of goat's cheese. Then pour enough egg mixture into each tin to bring it to the top of the tin. Add another slice of cheese and a cherry tomato to the top. Bake in the oven at 160°C (315°F/gas mark 5) for approximately 20 minutes or until set—firm to the touch. Remove from tin and serve with side salad.

mushroom and seafood quiche

Serves **4**

Ingredients
150 g (5 oz) plain white flour
pinch of salt
75 g (3 oz) hard margarine
cold water

Filling
1 small onion
2 or 3 large mushrooms
1 tablespoon oil
2 eggs
150 ml ($^1/_4$ pint) milk
seasoning—salt and pepper
50 g (2 oz) frozen prawns or fresh prawn tails
50 g (2 oz) grated cheddar cheese

Method
Sieve the flour and salt into a bowl. Cut in the margarine in cubes. Rub in the margarine with the tips of your fingers until mixture appears like fine breadcrumbs. Add enough cold water, dribble by dribble, to form the mixture into a ball of dough, using your hands. Sprinkle some flour onto a flat, preferably cold surface, and roll out the pastry. Roll out until big enough to fit a 20 cm (8 in) round tin comfortably. Place pastry in the tin and trim the excess from around the edges, using a knife. Set aside in the fridge or any cool place.

Method for filling
Dice the onion and mushrooms; then fry them together with the oil in a small pan for a few minutes, until tender. Beat the eggs in a jug, add the milk, and beat once more. Now add the fried onions and mushrooms. Season by adding a pinch of salt and pepper. Pour this mixture into the tin, scatter the prawns around the mixture and spread the grated cheese on top. Set the round tin onto a flat baking tray to catch any spills. Place in a preheated moderate oven (140°–160°C/275°–315°F/gas mark 5), for 30 minutes or until set. Pie should be firm to the touch and golden on top. Slice into wedges and serve with salad or on its own.

pan-fried fillet of lemon sole with citrus butter

Serves 4

Ingredients

8 fillets of lemon sole, 2 per person
2 tablespoons white flour
seasoning—pepper and salt
1 tablespoon vegetable oil
100 g (4 oz) butter
1 tablespoon lemon juice
1 dessertspoon chopped parsley
16 new potatoes

Method

Wash and dry fish. Place flour on a plate and season with pepper and salt. Place fish on flour and turn over. Pat off excess flour. In a medium frying pan, heat the vegetable oil and half of the butter until frothing. Add fillets of fish carefully, presentation side (fleshy side) down first. Fry until golden for approximately 3 minutes and then turn over and fry the other side for approximately 2 minutes. Remove to a warm plate. Add the other half of the butter to the pan, and allow it to heat up. Add the lemon juice and swirl around the pan. Pour the lemon butter over the fish on warm plates, and sprinkle with chopped parsley. Boil the potatoes for 8–10 minutes. Drain and pop 4 on each plate.

brochette of fresh prawns with sweet chilli sauce and pilaff rice

Serves ❹

Ingredients

2 cups long-grain rice
1 tablespoon vegetable oil
$^1/_2$ cup chopped green pepper
$^1/_2$ cup chopped red pepper
$^1/_2$ cup chopped yellow pepper
(If you don't like peppers, use petits pois, sweet corn and courgette, chopped finely.)
1 clove garlic (crushed or creamed)

2 button mushrooms finely chopped
4 cups chicken stock or water
1 dessertspoon chopped dill and parsley seasoning—pepper and salt
4 raw tiger prawns per person (alternatively cooked tiger prawns)
4 brochettes or skewers
3 tablespoons sweet chilli sauce
1 tablespoon vegetable oil

Method

To make the pilaff rice, rinse the rice thoroughly by running plenty of cold water through it to remove the excess starch. Heat the oil in a frying pan or saucepan and add all the chopped vegetables and garlic. Sauté them on medium heat for a few minutes. Now add the rice and stir to mix it in well with the vegetables. Fry this for 2 minutes or so, until the rice starts to change colour from clear to white. Add the stock or water and bring the whole lot to the boil. Lower the heat and simmer with the lid on for approximately 20 minutes, or until the rice is *aldente* and all the liquid has been absorbed. Now stir in the chopped dill and parsley and season with salt and pepper. This can be served hot or cold.

Soak the brochettes or skewers in cold water for 5 minutes before use to prevent them from burning. Thread the prawns onto the brochettes or skewers, and rub the prawns over generously with the sweet chilli sauce. Heat the oil in a frying pan, then cook the prawns on one side for 2 minutes. Turn over and cook the other side for a further 2 minutes. Remove from the heat and rub over again with the sweet chilli sauce. Serve on a bed of pilaff rice. These prawns are ideal for grilling or barbecuing also.

sweet potato savoury crumble

Serves **4**

Ingredients

1 tablespoon olive oil

1 medium onion

1 clove garlic

500 g (17 oz) minced round steak

1 teaspoon flour

1 teaspoon tomato purée

$^{1}/_{2}$ cup chopped tinned or fresh tomatoes

1 tablespoon water (optional)

1 teaspoon chopped thyme and parsley or

1 teaspoon mixed herbs

Sweet potato mash

2 sweet potatoes

25g butter

pepper

1 dessertspoon chopped basil

Savoury crumble

1 cup brown breadcrumbs

1 dessertspoon chopped parsley

25 g (1 oz) melted butter

seasoning—pepper and salt

Method

Heat the oil in a saucepan. Add the chopped onion and garlic, and sauté for a few minutes. Add the mined beef and break up well with a wooden spoon. Cook until the mince turns beige and add the flour. Add the tomato purée and tinned tomatoes and stock or water. Stir well, then add seasoning and herbs. Bring to the boil and simmer for 15 minutes. Place in a casserole dish. Top with mashed sweet potato and then with brown bread crumble. Place in a moderate oven (160°C/350°F/gas mark 5) for approximately 10 minutes to crisp topping.

Method for sweet potato mash

Wash and peel the sweet potatoes. Cut into chunks, place in a saucepan and cover with boiling water and a pinch of salt. Bring to the boil and simmer for 10 minutes or until soft. Strain, then add butter, pepper and chopped basil. Mash with a masher. Place on top of base and spread out.

Method for savoury crumble

Place breadcrumbs in a bowl. Add chopped parsley and melted butter. Mix well. Scatter on top of sweet potatoes.

chicken mughal and wild rice

Serves **4**

Ingredients
4 chicken breasts
1 clove garlic, crushed
3 cm (1^1/$_4$ in) piece of ginger chopped
1 teaspoon ground turmeric
^{1}/$_2$ teaspoon strands of saffron or ^{1}/$_4$ teaspoon powdered saffron
3 teaspoons garam masala
4 tablespoons hot milk
2 tablespoons vegetable oil
1 medium onion, sliced
pinch of salt
150 ml (6 fl oz) hot water
1 tablespoon ground almonds
150 ml (6 fl oz) cream
2 tablespoons chopped coriander
to serve: **wild rice or naan bread**

Method
Wash and dry the chicken breasts and cut into cubes. Place the garlic and all the spices in a bowl and add the hot milk. Mix well. Add the chicken pieces and stir until well coated. Allow to marinate for 30 minutes or so. Heat the vegetable oil in a saucepan and add the sliced onion. Cook until golden brown. Remove to a plate. Add the chicken pieces to the pan and cook until coloured, making sure all the spices are in the pan. Add salt and water and half of the cooked onions. Cook on a low heat for approximately 30 minutes. Remove the chicken to a warm serving plate. Add the ground almonds and cream to the pan and stir well. Cook over a low heat for 2–3 minutes until sauce thickens. Spoon over the chicken and serve garnished with the remaining onions and chopped coriander. Serve on a bed of wild rice or with naan bread as an accompaniment. Wild rice needs to be cooked for 30 minutes longer than ordinary rice.

spinach and ricotta cannelloni

Serves ❹

Ingredients
4 cannelloni tubes or 4 lasagne sheets
250 g (9 oz) spinach
1 tablespoon olive oil
1 clove garlic (creamed or crushed)
$^1/_2$ teaspoon ground nutmeg
seasoning—pepper and salt
1 tub (250 g/9 oz) ricotta cheese
a blob of pesto

béchamel sauce (see page 193)

to serve: mixed salad or tomato salad

Method
Soften the cannelloni tubes or the lasagne sheets by placing them in a bowl, pouring boiling water over them and allowing them to soak for 5 minutes. Remove and dry. If the spinach is the already-washed variety, place the bag and all in the microwave, turn on to high for 3 minutes, then remove and allow to cool. If it is freshly picked spinach, wash it and place in a saucepan, cover with boiling water and a teaspoon of salt, then bring to the boil and cook for 3 minutes. Drain and chop it finely. Place in a bowl.

Heat the olive oil in a frying pan and add the creamed garlic. Cook for 1 minute then add to the spinach in the bowl. Add the nutmeg and season with salt and pepper. Add the ricotta cheese and mix well.

Place the cannelloni or lasagne sheets on a greased casserole dish and spoon in the spinach mixture. Pour the béchamel sauce over the top and bake in a moderate oven (140°–160°C/275°–315°F/gas mark 5) until bubbling. Place a blob of pesto on the top immediately before serving. Serve with mixed salad or tomato salad.

beef curry

Serves ❹

Ingredients

500 g (17 oz) boneless rib steak
1 medium onion
1 clove garlic
1 tablespoon vegetable oil
1 teaspoon mild or hot curry powder
$^1/_2$ teaspoon garam masala
$^1/_2$ teaspoon cardamom powder
1 dessertspoon white flour
1 teaspoon tomato purée
750 ml (1$^1/_4$ pint) brown stock or water
3 teaspoons tomato and apple chutney (can be bought)
seasoning—salt and pepper
to serve: plain white rice

Method

Wash and dry the meat and cut into narrow slanting pieces, then set aside. Peel and chop the onion finely. Cream or crush the garlic. In a medium saucepan, heat the oil. Add the onion and garlic and sauté for a few minutes, then add the curry powder, garam masala, cardamom and flour. Stir well and cook for 1 minute before adding the tomato purée. Remove from the heat and add the stock or water slowly, stirring all the time. Return to the heat and bring to the boil. Now add the meat, chutney and seasoning. Lower the heat and simmer for approximately 30 minutes or until the meat is tender. Serve with cooked plain white rice.

To cook rice

Measure the rice by the cup. For 4 people, use 2 cups of rice. Place in a saucepan and add 4 cups of cold water. Bring to the boil and simmer with the lid off for approximately 15 minutes or until *aldente*. Do not stir during cooking. Strain through a sieve, then pour hot water over it to wash away any excess starch. For more tips, see the kitchen tips section (page 28).

beef cannelloni with tomato sauce

Serves **4**

Ingredients
4 cannelloni tubes or 4 lasagne sheets
1 tablespoon olive oil
1 medium onion, finely chopped
1 clove garlic (creamed or crushed)
400 g (14 oz) minced round steak
1 teaspoon tomato purée
1 teaspoon flour
1 teaspoon Italian seasoning
$^{1}/_{2}$ tin chopped tomatoes
1 tablespoon freshly chopped basil
1 tablespoon freshly grated Parmesan
seasoning—pepper and salt
tomato sauce (see page 193)

Method
Soften the cannelloni tubes or the lasagne sheets by placing them in a bowl, pouring boiling water over them and allowing them to soak for 5 minutes. Remove and dry. Heat the olive oil in a saucepan, then add the finely chopped onion and the garlic and sauté for a few minutes. Add the minced beef, making sure to break it up well. Cook over a moderate heat until it turns beige. Add the tomato purée, flour and Italian seasoning. Stir well, then add the chopped tomatoes and basil. Bring to the boil, then lower heat and allow to simmer for 10 minutes. Add seasoning.

Carefully fill the cannelloni tubes with the mixture. If you are using the lasagne sheets, spoon the mixture on top and roll up into a sausage shape. Place them side by side on a greased casserole dish. Pour the tomato sauce over the top and sprinkle with Parmesan cheese. Bake in a moderate oven (140°–160°C/275°–315°F/gas mark 5) for approximately 30 minutes. Serve with a selection of mixed salad leaves.

roast chicken with mediterranean vegetables

Serves ❹

Ingredients
1 chicken (1,400g or 3lb)
olive oil to rub over
seasoning—salt and pepper
4 medium potatoes

Gravy
1 tablespoon flour
pepper and salt
125 ml (4¹/₂ fl oz) brown stock or water

Method
Wipe chicken with kitchen tissue. Rub over with olive oil, then sprinkle with salt and pepper. Preheat the oven to 160°C (315°F/gas mark 5). Place the roasting pan in the oven to heat it. When it is hot, place the chicken on it, *breast side down*. Cook for 15 minutes. Turn over and allow it to roast for a further hour or until the juices run clear when you pierce the leg with a skewer or knife. To roast potatoes with the chicken, wash and peel them, then parboil them in a saucepan of boiling salted water for 5 minutes and drain before putting them in the pan with the chicken. Add the potatoes to the chicken during its cooking, allowing 40 minutes' cooking time for them. Once the chicken and potatoes are done, remove them both from the roasting dish to a plate and keep warm.

Method for the gravy
To make the gravy, take the roasting pan in which the chicken was roasted, sprinkle the flour and some pepper and salt onto it, and add the brown stock or water. Place on a ring on the stove-top and bring to the boil, stirring well to make sure that all of the sediment from the pan is dissolved into the mixture. Simmer for 5 minutes, then strain into a warm jug or spoon over the chicken when serving.

mediterranean vegetables

Ingredients

1 green pepper
1 yellow pepper
1 red pepper
1 courgette
1 parsnip
12 cherry tomatoes
2 tablespoons olive oil
1 clove garlic (creamed or crushed)
to serve: **torn basil leaves, if desired**

Method

Cut each of the peppers into four pieces, removing the stem, pith and seeds. Cut the top and bottom off the courgette and cut into generous chunks. Peel and chop the parsnip into wedges. Place all the above, along with the cherry tomatoes, in a bowl with the olive oil and the crushed garlic, coating the vegetables well. Place in a roasting dish or on a baking tray. Cook in a moderate oven (140°–160°C/275°–315°F/gas mark 4–5) for 10 minutes, then turn them all over and cook for a further 10 minutes. Serve on a large plate and sprinkle with torn basil leaves, if desired.

brochette of lamb, red onion and aubergine, on a bed of colcannon

Serves 4

Ingredients

400 g (14 oz) cubed lamb, either shoulder or leg (This can be bought already cut up at the butcher's.)
2 red onions, each cut into quarters
1 aubergine, cubed
seasoning—salt and pepper
4 brochettes or skewers

Marinade

$^1/_2$ cup olive oil
1 dessertspoon red wine vinegar
1 dessertspoon soy sauce
1 clove garlic (creamed or crushed)
$^1/_4$ teaspoon grain mustard

Method

Mix all the ingredients for the marinade together in a bowl. Add the lamb and mix until meat is entirely coated. Cover and place in the fridge to marinate overnight. Thread the lamb, onion and aubergine onto metal skewers or wooden skewers which have been soaked in water (this prevents burning). Put 4 pieces of meat and 2 each of the onion and aubergine on each skewer. Season with salt and pepper. Place on a greased baking tray and roast in a moderate oven (140°–160°C/275°–315°F/gas mark 4–5) for 10 minutes. Turn over and continue to cook until meat is tender. Serve with colcannon.

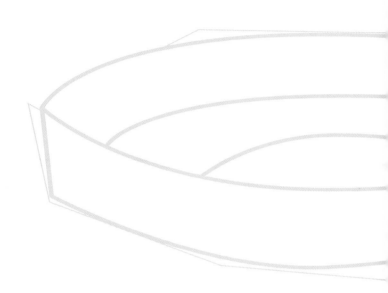

colcannon

Ingredients
4 medium red rooster potatoes
$^1/_2$ teaspoon salt
300 g (11 oz) raw curly kale or green cabbage
1 small onion finely chopped
25 g (1 oz) melted butter
seasoning—pepper and salt

Method
Wash, peel and cut potatoes into 4 pieces. Place in a saucepan and cover with boiling water. Add $^1/_2$ teaspoon of salt, and bring to the boil. Turn down to simmer for 15 minutes until tender. In the meantime, cook the kale or cabbage by first washing and de-veining it, then placing it in a saucepan and covering it with boiling, lightly salted water. Bring it to the boil, then let it simmer for 5 minutes. Strain it, and then chop it finely. Once the potatoes are cooked through, strain the excess fluid from them. Return them to the saucepan and mash them well using a hand masher. Now add the chopped onion, curly kale and melted butter and season with pepper and salt. Mix well and voilà!

4

desserts

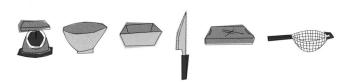

chocolate and pear crumble

Serves ❹

Ingredients
100 g (4 oz) plain white flour
50 g (2 oz) hard margarine
50 g (2 oz) caster sugar
1 packet chocolate buttons
Filling: 4 pears or 1 tin of pear halves (drained)

Method
Sieve the flour into a bowl and rub in the margarine with your fingertips until the mixture looks like fine breadcrumbs. Add the sugar and chopped chocolate buttons. Peel and slice the pears and place them in a greased pie dish. Top the pears with the crumble mixture. Leave the mixture loose—do not press down. Bake in a pre-heated, moderate oven (140°–160°C/275°–315°F/gas mark 4–5) until the crumble is golden brown. Serve warm with whipped cream.

rhubarb, orange and ginger crumble

Serves ❹

Ingredients
150 g (6 oz) plain white flour
75 g (3 oz) hard margarine
75 g (3 oz) sugar
Filling: 4 sticks rhubarb
grated rind and juice of 1 orange
$^1/_2$ teaspoon ground ginger
1 dessertspoon sugar to sweeten

Method
Sieve flour into a bowl and rub in margarine with your fingertips until the mixture looks like fine breadcrumbs. Add the sugar and mix well. Chop the rhubarb. Place rhubarb, orange and ginger in a pie dish. Sprinkle with sugar and top with the crumble mixture. Bake in a moderate oven (140°–160°C/275°–315°F/gas mark 4–5) until the crumble is golden brown. Serve warm with whipped cream.

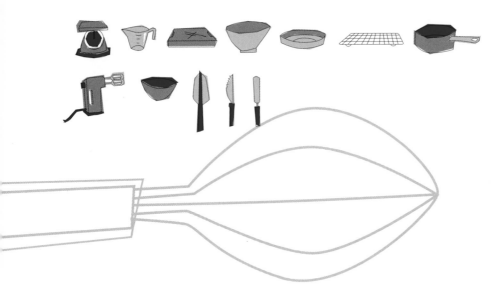

strawberry cake

Ingredients
50 g (2 oz) soft margarine
50 g (2 oz) caster sugar
75 g (3 oz) self-raising flour
1 egg (medium)
Filling: 150 ml (¹/₄ pint) whipping cream
6 strawberries
50 g (2 oz) cooking chocolate to make 10 chocolate squares (see method below)

Method
Put the margarine, sugar, flour and egg in a bowl. With an electric mixer, beat them all
together until mixture is creamy. If the mixture is too stiff, add a desertspoon of milk at
this stage. Pour mixture into a greased 18 cm (7 in) sandwich tin and bake at 170°C
(325°F/gas mark 5) for 15 minutes or until golden brown. Turn onto a wire tray and allow
to cool. Place on a decorative plate. Top with the whipped cream, spreading it out carefully,
and decorate with strawberries and chocolate squares.

Method for chocolate squares
Place cooking chocolate in a bowl and over a saucepan of hot water and allow to melt.
Lay a sheet of greaseproof paper on a flat surface. Spread the melted chocolate onto the
paper, thinly and evenly. When the chocolate sets, cut it into equal squares.

To make a double-layer cake, simply double the cake mixture and bake in 2 tins. Sandwich
together with strawberries and whipped cream between the layers.

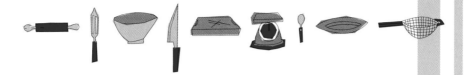

apple tart

Ingredients
150 g (6 oz) plain white flour
75 g (3 oz) margarine
pinch of salt
cold water

Filling
2 medium cooking apples
sugar to taste
$^1/_2$ teaspoon of ground cloves or cinnamon (optional)
to finish: a little beaten egg

Method
To make the pastry, sieve the flour into a bowl. Rub in the margarine with the tips of your fingers until mixture appears like fine breadcrumbs. Add dribbles of cold water and knead with your hands until the mixture resembles a lump of playdoh. It should be neither sticky nor crumbly. (See page 26 for more tips on pastry making.) Sprinkle some flour onto a flat, cool surface and flour the rolling pin. Divide mixture into two equal pieces. Roll out each piece to fit a round 18 cm (7 in) ovenproof plate. Place one half on the plate and trim around the edges with a knife to neaten up the appearance. Put the other half aside.

Peel the apples. Remove and discard the cores and place the remainder of the apples on a chopping board. Cut each one in half, then slice as thinly as possible. Arrange the apple slices evenly on the pastry plate and sprinkle some sugar over the top. Arrange another layer over this and, if you wish, sprinkle a pinch of cinnamon or cloves evenly over the top also.

So that the pie will stay sealed, wet the edges of the pastry on the plate, using a pastry brush. Then place the top piece of pastry over the plate like a cap, and press the edges together. Using the pastry brush, rub over the whole pie with a little beaten egg. Decorate the edges and make a slit in the centre top to let out steam while cooking. Bake in a pre-heated oven: for the first 5 minutes at 180°C (350°F/gas mark 7), then reduce the heat to 170°C (325°F/gas mark 5) until the tart is cooked. The tart will have an overall golden brown appearance when it is ready; it usually takes between 30 and 40 minutes.

éclairs au chocolat

Serves **4**

Ingredients

Choux pastry
50 g (2 oz) hard margarine
125 ml (4^1/$_2$ fl oz) water
62 g (2^1/$_2$ oz) plain white flour
2 medium–sized eggs

Chocolate Glacé Icing
150 g (5 oz) icing sugar
1 dessertspoon cocoa
boiling water
for filling: 125 ml (4^1/$_2$ fl oz) whipping cream

Method

To make the pastry, place the margarine and water in a small saucepan and bring to the boil. Simmer until the margarine is completely melted. Remove from the heat. Sieve the flour into a bowl and add to the pot of water and melted margarine. Beat well. Allow this mixture to cool completely. Add the eggs, one at a time, beating the mixture well with an electric mixer before adding the next egg. All of this can be done in the original pot, or, if you prefer, you can do it in a bowl. Place the mixture in a plain icing bag and, using a medium-sized nozzle, pipe the mixture out onto a well-greased tin. Pipe out fingers of the mixture approximately 8 cm (3 in) long. If you do not have an icing bag, use a dessertspoon to spoon out mixture in blobs onto the tin. Place in a hot oven (180°C–200°C/350°F–400°F/gas mark 7–8) for 5 minutes. Reduce to moderate oven (140°–160°C/275°–315°F/gas mark 5–6) and continue to bake until dried out (approximately 15 minutes). Remove from oven and immediately slit a hole in one side of each puff. Allow to cool completely on a wire tray.

For the filling, simply whip the cream in a bowl and spoon or pipe through the slit into the middle of the éclair puff. Pipe or spoon on the chocolate glacé icing.

Method for icing

Sieve the icing sugar and cocoa together into a bowl. Add dribble by dribble of hot water very slowly until the icing is the right consistency. It should be shiny and easy to spoon over the éclairs, but not runny. It is very easy to get the mixture too wet—just a drop too much water can do it. But it's an easy fix! If the mixture is too runny, simply add a little more icing sugar and cocoa to it to thicken it up.

chocolate mousse

This is a very simple recipe, but don't be fooled by that—it makes the most delicious mousse you will ever taste!

Serves ❹

Ingredients
3 eggs
150 g (5 oz) Bourneville chocolate (dark cooking chocolate is also fine)

Method
Separate the eggs, putting the whites in a Pyrex bowl and the yolks in a cup, and leave aside. Break up chocolate into pieces and put in another tempered glass (Pyrex) bowl, then place the bowl over a saucepan of simmering hot water and stir until the chocolate has melted. Beat the egg whites with an electric mixer until stiff—this means that the whites stand up in stiff peaks and will not pour out of the bowl when turned upside down. Add the yolks to the melted chocolate and stir briskly. Using a balloon whisk, fold in the stiffly beaten egg whites and stir gently and continually, until mixture is smooth. Don't delay. Work quickly when folding egg whites. Pour the mixture into four wine glasses and leave in the fridge to set and until ready to eat.

chocolate cake with fudge icing

Ingredients
125 g (5 oz) plain white flour
25 g (1 oz) cocoa
1 teaspoon baking powder
150 g (6 oz) soft margarine
150 g (6 oz) caster sugar
3 eggs

Fudge Icing
500 g (18 oz) icing sugar
1 tablespoon cocoa
50 g (2 oz) margarine or butter
hot water
to decorate: flaked chocolate or chocolate buttons

Method
Sieve flour, cocoa and baking powder into a bowl. Add remaining ingredients and beat with a mixer until light and fluffy—about 5 minutes. Divide mixture in half and pour into two well-greased 20 cm (8 in) cake tins. Bake in a moderate oven (140°–160°C/275°–315°F/gas mark 4–5) for 30 minutes or until cooked. Remove cakes from the tins and place on a wire tray to cool. Make the fudge icing while you are waiting.

Method for fudge icing
Sieve the icing sugar and cocoa into a bowl. Melt the margarine and add to the mixture. Add, dribble-by-dribble, enough hot water to the mixture until it is smooth but not runny.

Spread half of the icing on one layer of the cake. Place the second layer on top, to make a sandwich. Smooth the rest of the icing over the top and down the sides, covering completely. To smooth icing evenly, dip a knife in hot water and spread out. Decorate with some flaked chocolate or chocolate buttons.

chocolate chip shortbread cookies

Ingredients
50 g (2 oz) cooking chocolate or chocolate chips
200 g (7 oz) plain white flour
$^1/_2$ teaspoon baking powder
100 g (4 oz) hard margarine
100 g (4 oz) caster sugar
1 egg
1 teaspoon vanilla essence

Method
If you are using block chocolate, chop it up into small chips. Sieve the flour and baking powder into a bowl and rub in the margarine until mixture resembles fine breadcrumbs. Add the chocolate and sugar. Beat the egg and vanilla essence together in a cup, and add to the mixture. Mix well with your hands. Place the mixture on a floured surface or board and, using your hands, knead the mixture with closed fists until it makes a smooth ball. Cut the mixture into two halves and roll each half out to about a 1 cm ($^1/_2$ in) depth. Use a cookie cutter to stamp out your cookies. Place them on a greased baking tray and prick the tops with a fork. Bake in a moderate oven (140°–160°C/275°–315°F/gas mark 4–5) for 15–20 minutes or until nicely golden. Remove from the oven and place on a wire tray until cool. Store in an airtight container.

almond biscuits

Makes **16**

Ingredients

100 g (4 oz) soft margarine
150 g (6 oz) plain white flour
100 g (4 oz) caster sugar
¹/₂ beaten egg

1 teaspoon baking powder
1 drop almond essence
topping: 16 almonds or chocolate buttons for the top

Method

Place all the ingredients in a bowl, except for the topping. Mix well. With your hands, break off mixture and roll into small balls. Flatten slightly so that they do not roll around, then place an almond or button on top. Brush over the top with the beaten egg, using a pastry brush. Place on a greased baking tray, leaving plenty of space between each one for them to spread out. Bake in a moderate oven (140°–160°C/275°–315°F/gas mark 4–5) for 15–20 minutes or until golden. Remove from the oven and place on a cooling tray. Store in an airtight container.

cookie surprise

Ingredients

275 ml (¹/₂ pint) whipping cream
1 packet chocolate chip cookies or ginger snaps
3 tablespoons orange juice or rum (optional)
1 chocolate flake or 1 packet Smarties or fresh fruit to decorate

Method

Whip the cream in a jug or bowl until soft, not too stiff. Dip the cookies in the orange juice or rum. Use a blob of cream to sandwich them together, and arrange them back to back on a decorative plate in a log formation. Completely cover the cookie log with the rest of the whipped cream. To decorate, sprinkle the crushed flake over the top. Alternatively, dot with Smarties or decorate with fresh fruit of your choice. This is a fun dessert to look at so use your imagination when decorating. At Christmas, it can be used for young people as a simple alternative to plum pudding.

frosted carrot cake

Ingredients
100 g (4 oz) margarine
100 g (4 oz) brown sugar
150 g (5 oz) plain white flour
1 teaspoon mixed spice
$^1/_2$ teaspoon ground ginger
2 teaspoons baking powder
2 eggs
2 tablespoons orange juice
rind of $^1/_2$ orange
100 g (4 oz) grated carrot

Frosting
75 g (3 oz) icing sugar
50 g (2 oz) cream cheese
25 g (1 oz) soft margarine
a little grated orange rind
1 dessertspoon of orange juice

Method
Using an electric mixer, cream the margarine and sugar together until fluffy. Sieve in the flour, mixed spice, ground ginger and baking powder. Beat the two eggs, add to the mixture and mix well. Stir in the orange juice, orange rind and grated carrot. Pour the mixture into a well-greased 900 g (2 lb) loaf tin. Bake in a moderate oven (140°–160°C/275°–315°F/gas mark 4–5) for 40 minutes or until cooked. Remove from oven and place on a wire tray to cool. While the cake is cooling, place all the frosting ingredients in a bowl and mix together. Spread frosting over the top of the cake when it is cool. This cake is inclined to break easily, so slice carefully with a bread knife.

lemon cake with frosting

Ingredients
100 g (4 oz) soft margarine
100 g (4 oz) caster sugar
150 g (5 oz) self-raising white flour
rind of 1 lemon and the juice of $^1/_2$ lemon
2 eggs
2 drops of lemon essence

Frosting
50 g (2 oz) cream cheese
25 g (1 oz) icing sugar
1 dessertspoon lemon juice (drizzle in, using a teaspoon)
25 g (1 oz) soft margarine or butter
to decorate: half slices of lemon

Method
Place all the cake ingredients in a bowl and beat well with an electric mixer. When mixture
is smooth and creamy, spoon into a well-greased 900 g (2 lb) loaf tin and spread evenly.
Bake in a moderate oven (140°–160°C/275°–315°F/gas mark 4–5) for 40 minutes or until
a skewer comes out clean. Remove from oven and place on cooling tray.

Method for frosting
Mix all the ingredients together well. Spread over the top of the cake when cool. Decorate
with half slices of lemon, twisted in the middle.

danish strawberry shortcake

Ingredients

Pastry

100 g (4 oz) plain white flour
30 g (1¹/₄ oz) icing sugar
75 g (3 oz) butter or margarine
1 egg yolk
3 drops vanilla essence

Filling

1 punnet strawberries
275 ml (¹/₂ pint) whipping cream

Jam glaze

2 tablespoons strawberry jam
1 dessertspoon water

Method

Sieve flour into a bowl on top of all of the rest of the pastry ingredients. Using your hands, knead the mixture together until a ball is formed. Chill for 30 minutes. To chill, put the ball in greaseproof paper or cling film and place it in the fridge. Using a floured rolling pin, roll out the pastry into a 20 cm (8 in) circle and place it on a well-greased flat baking sheet. Prick it with a fork and bake in a moderate oven (140°–160°C/275°–315°F/gas mark 4–5) for 10–15 minutes or until golden. Cool and place on a plate. Make the jam glaze and brush over the strawberries. Cover the cooked pastry with whipped cream.
Place glazed strawberries on top, bottoms up.

Method for jam glaze

Place jam and water in a saucepan and boil up. Strain through a sieve and use while still warm. Caution: hot jam glaze can give a bad burn.

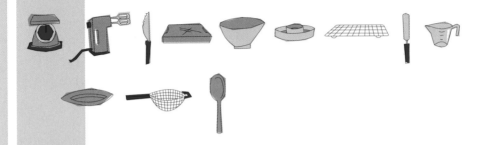

strawberry and cream flan

Ingredients
2 eggs
50 g (2 oz) caster sugar
50 g (2 oz) plain white flour

For topping
1 punnet strawberries
275 ml (¹/₂ pint) whipped cream
chocolate squares*

Method
Beat eggs and sugar together in a bowl with an electric mixer, until thick and creamy. Sieve the flour over the top of the mixture, and fold together. With a spoon, pour mixture into a 20 cm (8 in) well-greased flan tin and bake in a moderate oven (140°–160°C/275°–315°F/gas mark 4–5) for approximately 20 minutes.

Turn out onto a cooling tray and, when cool, transfer onto a decorative plate. Whip the cream in a jug with an electric mixer. Fill the flan with whipped cream and top with strawberries and chocolate squares. If you like, decorate with rosettes of cream using a piping bag with a rose nozzle attached.

*For chocolate squares, melt some cooking chocolate and spread it on some greaseproof paper. Cut into squares when hard.

raspberry sorbet

Serves ❹

Ingredients
1 tablespoon sugar
150 ml (¹/₄ pint) cold water
1 carton fresh or frozen raspberries
1 egg white
to decorate: sprig of mint or crumbled chocolate flake

Method
Place the sugar and water in a small saucepan. Allow the sugar to dissolve and slowly bring the mixture to the boil. Turn down the heat. Pop in the raspberries and allow to simmer for 5 minutes. Pour the mixture into a bowl and leave to cool. Once the mixture is cool, blend until smooth in the liquidiser. Pour into a plastic bowl with a cover and place in the freezer for 40 minutes. The mixture will now be half-frozen. Remove from freezer and empty back into the liquidiser and blend again for about 30 seconds. Place back in the plastic bowl and return to the freezer for another 40 minutes. Beat the egg white until it stands up in stiff peaks. After the 40 minutes have elapsed, take the mixture out of the freezer once more and empty back into the liquidiser. Liquidise for 15 seconds then place in bowl with the stiff egg whites. Fold these together until they are evenly mixed in. Return mixture to the freezer until ready to serve.

To serve, heat the ice-cream scooper (or a spoon) in very hot water, then scoop out the mixture and place each scoop into a wine glass. Add a sprig of mint to the top or a crumbled chocolate flake to make it extra yummy.

scrummy squares

Ingredients
300 g (11 oz) plain white flour
50 g (2 oz) cornflakes
50 g (2 oz) desiccated coconut
100 g (4 oz) caster sugar
2 tablespoons cocoa powder
1 teaspoon baking powder
pinch of salt
200 g (7 oz) hard margarine or butter
150 g (5 oz) cooking chocolate

Method
Place the flour, cornflakes, coconut, caster sugar, cocoa powder, baking powder and salt in a bowl and mix well. Melt the butter or margarine in a pot or in the microwave. Add the melted butter or margarine to the dry mixture slowly, making sure to mix it in well until you have achieved a uniform colour and texture. Pour the mixture out onto a flat baking tray and mash down flat using the back of a dessertspoon. Bake in a moderate oven (140°–160°C/275°–315°F/gas mark 4–5) for 10–12 minutes. Remove and cool. Melt the cooking chocolate (see page 16). Pour over the top of the pan of cookies and smooth out over the entire surface area. Cool. Cut into squares and serve!

You can substitute the cornflakes with rice crispies. If you decide to do this, leave out the cocoa also.

chocolate pecan pie

Ingredients
100 g (4 oz) plain white flour
pinch of salt
50 g (2 oz) butter or hard margarine
cold water

Filling
4 large eggs
100g (4 oz) caster sugar
$^3/_4$ cup corn syrup or $^1/_2$ cup golden syrup
1 tablespoon melted butter
200 g (8 oz) chopped pecans
100 g (4 oz) chopped chocolate
2 teaspoons cocoa
1 tablespoon white flour
1 teaspoon vanilla essence
to decorate: 4 whole pecans

Method
Grease a 20 cm (8 in) loose-based sandwich tin. For the pastry base, sieve the flour and salt into a bowl. Cut in the butter or margarine and rub in with the tips of your fingers, until the mixture resembles fine breadcrumbs. Add enough cold water, dribble by dribble, to make the pastry into a ball of dough. Sprinkle flour out on a flat surface and place the ball of dough on it. Using a floured rolling pin, roll the dough out until it will fit the greased tin. Carefully place into the tin and cut away any excess dough from around the edges. Put in the fridge while you prepare the filling.

Method for filling
Break the eggs into a bowl. Add the caster sugar and whisk until well mixed and creamy. Add the rest of the filling ingredients and stir well. Pour on top of the pastry base. Place the four pecans in the centre in a flower shape. Bake in a preheated oven at about 150°C (300°F/gas mark 4) for approximately 40 minutes or until firm to the touch. Allow to cool in the tin. Turn out when completely cooled. Serve in wedges with a scoop of ice cream or fresh cream or simply on its own.

almond fingers

Makes ❻

Ingredients
150 g (6 oz) plain white flour
pinch of salt
¹/₂ teaspoon baking powder
75 g (3 oz) hard margarine or butter
75 g (3 oz) caster sugar
1 egg yolk
2 drops almond essence
1 tablespoon water (approximately)

Topping
2 tablespoons apricot jam (or other, if preferred)
1 egg white
3 dessertspoons caster sugar
2 tablespoons chopped almonds

Method
Grease an 18 cm x 28 cm (7 in x 8 in) baking tin—known as a Yorkshire tin. Sieve the flour, salt and baking powder into a bowl. Using your fingertips, rub in the margarine until the mixture resembles fine breadcrumbs. Add the caster sugar and mix together again. Add the egg yolk, almond essence and approximately 1 tablespoon of cold water—enough to form the mixture into a ball. Flour your hands well, then press the mixture into the tin. Press it out evenly into the corners. Prick over with a fork. Bake at 160°C (315°F/gas mark 4–5) for 15 minutes. Spread with the jam while still hot.

Prepare the rest of the topping by stiffly beating the egg white until it stands up in peaks. Add the caster sugar, a little at a time, continuing to beat the egg white all the time. This is a meringue mixture. Spread the egg white over the top of the cookie dough and jam. Sprinkle the chopped almonds evenly over the top also and return all to the oven. Reduce the heat to 140°C (275°F/gas mark 2) and bake for a further 10 minutes or until the meringue is golden. Remove from the oven and allow to cool in the tin. Cut in two lengthways, then into six fingers. Store in an airtight container.

peanut butter cookies

Makes **10**

Ingredients
grated rind of 1 orange
50 g (2 oz) butter or soft margarine
50 g (2 oz) caster sugar
2 tablespoons brown sugar
1 egg
100 g (4 oz) self-raising flour
3 tablespoons smooth peanut butter

Method
Clean the orange then grate it to get the rind. Place in a bowl with the butter or margarine
and the sugar. Using an electric mixer, beat well for a few minutes. Add the egg and flour,
then beat again until well mixed in. Add the peanut butter and mix in slowly until well
combined together. Using your hands, divide the mixture into 10 balls. Press down on the
top of each ball slightly so that it will not roll. Place the balls an inch or two apart on a flat
greased baking tray and mark with the top of a fork. Bake in a moderate oven
(170°C/325°F/gas mark 4–5) for 25 minutes, or until golden brown. Remove from oven
and place on a wire tray to cool. Store in an airtight container.

fresh fruit kebabs

Makes ❹

Ingredients
juice of 1 orange
juice of ¹/₂ lemon
1 tablespoon sugar
1 orange
2 bananas
2 slices pineapple
8 green or red grapes
1 pear
1 red apple
1 dessertspoon honey (runny preferably)

Method
Soak four kebab sticks or wooden skewers in cold water—this prevents them from burning under the grill. Place the orange and lemon juice in a bowl. Add the sugar and stir well. Peel the orange and separate into segments. Peel the bananas and cut each into 4 pieces. Cut the pineapple into chunks. Remove the seeds from the grapes. Place all of the fruit in the bowl and stir well. Skewer a mixture of fruits onto the kebab sticks or skewers. Using a pastry brush, rub them with the honey, then place them on a flat baking tray lined with tin foil. Preheat the grill and place the kebabs under it. Cook until they have sizzled, then turn them over and allow the other side to sizzle. Remove and serve immediately. These are light, healthy and divine. Lovely on their own or with a dollop of ice-cream. Assorted cubed melon may also be used.

pink meringue bowls

Serves ❹

Ingredients
3 egg whites
pinch of salt
150 g (5 oz) caster sugar
1 or 2 drops of pink food colouring (cochineal)

Method
Preheat the oven to 90°C (195°F/gas mark ¹/₂). Line a baking tray with greaseproof paper. Place the egg whites in a tempered glass (Pyrex) or delph bowl. Make sure that there is absolutely no yolk in the whites! The fat that is contained in the yolk will make the meringues collapse. This is why greaseproof paper is used and not a greased dish for meringues—any oil or fat coming in contact with them is disastrous! Add a pinch of salt. Using an electric mixer on high, whisk the egg whites until stiff. Add the sugar, a little at a time, beating all the time. The mixture is ready when it does not drip off the whisks. Only when completely finished using the electric beater, add the pink food colouring. Add one drop at a time and mix through gently with a metal spoon until a satisfactory pink colour is reached. Using two dessertspoons, spoon the mixture out onto the baking tray, shaping into a bowl or basket of your desired size. Place in the oven for approximately 1 hour or until completely dried out and crisp. Remove and place on a wire tray to cool. Serve filled with whipped cream and/or fresh fruit in season.

lemon mousse

Serves ❹

Ingredients
2 eggs
50 g (2 oz) sugar
1 lemon—grated rind and juice
1¹/₂ tablespoons cold water
1 dessertspoon powdered gelatine
to decorate: 4 half slices of lemon

Method
Separate the yolks and the whites of the eggs and place in separate bowls. Add the sugar and lemon rind to the yolks. Place the cold water in a cup with half of the lemon juice, then sprinkle the gelatine over the top and allow it to soak for a couple of minutes. Using an electric mixer, stiffly beat the egg whites to form peaks. Now beat the egg yolk mixture until thick and creamy. Dissolve the gelatine by placing the cup in a saucepan of hot water, or placing in the microwave for a few seconds until the mixture is totally clear and liquefied. You must work quickly once the gelatine is ready because it sets as it cools. Add it to the egg yolk mixture, beating all the time. Do not pour it in before you have begun beating as it will cool too fast and form into rubbery strings. Continue to beat the mixture for a few minutes more, then add the other half of the lemon juice and mix in well. Set aside the electric mixer. Add the stiffly beaten egg whites and, using a metal spoon, fold the two together gently until blended. Pour into four individual decorative glasses or dishes. Place in the fridge until set. Decorate with some lemon twists. This is a refreshing and healthy dessert.

caramelised bananas in crêpes

Makes **8**

Ingredients
Crêpe batter
100 g (4 oz) plain white flour
1 egg
250 ml (9 fl oz) milk
pinch of salt

Filling
50 g (2 oz) butter
50 g (2 oz) caster sugar
4 ripe bananas
to finish: sieved icing sugar, if desired

Method

Using an electric mixer, beat all the crêpe ingredients together in a bowl or jug, making sure that there are no lumps. Set aside for at least one hour. This amount makes approximately 8 crêpes.

To fry the crêpes, use a small non-stick omelette or crêpe pan. Lightly oil the pan, and allow it to get hot. It is easiest to use a jug to pour the mixture onto the pan. Pour enough mixture to cover the base of the pan with a thin film. You can adjust the thickness by pouring some in and then swishing the pan around to make the mixture run out and cover the base. This will give you nice thin crêpes. Allow to cook for approximately 2 minutes, until golden, then turn over and cook the other side until golden. Keep warm on a plate while finishing the other crêpes.

Method for filling

Once you have finished making the crêpes, wipe out the pan you have been using. Add to it the butter and caster sugar. Put it back on the heat until the sugar has dissolved. Cut the bananas in two lengthways and place them in the pan. Baste (spoon over with fluid) the bananas with the buttery sugar mixture until the sugar turns a little brown and the bananas are heated through.

To serve, place one crêpe on a serving plate. Put a half banana on top and roll up. Spoon some of the sauce from the pan over the top. Sieve a little icing sugar over the top if desired. Repeat for the remainder of the crêpes. Serve with a scoop of vanilla ice-cream. This recipe is also delicious using slices of mango rather than bananas.

sweet apple and almond cake

Ingredients
150 g (6 oz) soft margarine
150 g (6 oz) light brown sugar
150 g (6 oz) plain white flour
1 teaspoon baking powder
3 large eggs
1 teaspoon mixed spice

Filling/Topping
2 pink or Granny Smith eating apples
1 tablespoon brown sugar for the top
50 g (2 oz) flaked almonds

Method
Grease a 20 cm (8 in) loose-based round tin. Cut out a piece of greaseproof paper to fit the bottom of the tin and place inside. Preheat the oven to 160°C (315°F/gas mark 4–5). Place all of the cake ingredients in a bowl and beat well using an electric mixer until it is soft and creamy. Pour half of the mixture into the tin, smoothing out to the edges of the tin. Peel, core and slice one of the apples. Cover the cake mixture in the tin with slices of apple, then pour the other half of the mixture over the top. Smooth out the mixture to the edges of the tin. Slice the other apple with peel on and arrange in a nice pattern on top. Sprinkle the brown sugar and the flaked almonds over the top. Place in the oven to cook for approximately 40 minutes. To check if the cake is ready, pierce the centre of it with a skewer. If the skewer comes out clean (no wet dough on it), the cake is ready! Remove from the oven and allow to cool in the tin. Once cooled, remove from the tin and place on a decorative plate. Serve cut into wedges, hot or cold, on its own or with whipped cream or ice-cream.

Carrot cake

eve's oaties

Ingredients
125 g (4¹/₂ oz) butter at room temperature
85 g (3¹/₂ oz) sugar
1 teaspoon vanilla essence
100 g (4 oz) flour
¹/₂ teaspoon baking powder
¹/₂ teaspoon baking soda
120 g (4¹/₂ oz) oatmeal
1 tablespoon of boiling water

Method
Turn on the oven to 175°C (325°F/gas mark 5). Put the butter and sugar in a mixing bowl
and cream together using an electric mixer. Add the vanilla essence, followed by the flour,
baking powder and baking soda. Beat all the ingredients together. Throw in the oatmeal.
The mixture is probably very dry now, so add boiling water until it becomes stiff enough to
form into balls. You will need at least two baking sheets—there is no need to grease
them. Break off a little of the mixture and form into a ball. Now press the ball flat, with
your hands together, to form a cookie. Pop onto the baking sheet. Leave a space around
each cookie as they spread in baking. Continue this until you have used up the mixture.
If your kitchen is very warm and the mixture seems too sticky, pop it in the fridge for an
hour before you want to bake them. These are delicious and so easy.

5

grab grub

Brochette of fresh prawns with sweet chilli sauce

Pan-fried fillet of lemon sole with citrus butter

Stuffed green peppers with ratatouille

Beef curry

Oriental pork with noodles

Beef cannelloni with tomato sauce

Lamb shish kebabs with raita & spicy cous cous

Chicken mughal and wild rice

Sweet red pepper soup

Potato cubes with bacon & balsamic dressing

sss secret salad sandwiches

Makes 4 rounds of sandwiches

Ingredients
8 slices white or brown sliced pan
2 spring onions
2 medium tomatoes
2 cups shredded lettuce
2 hard boiled eggs
1 cup grated cheddar cheese
1 medium carrot
2 tablespoons mayonnaise
seasoning

> **Carrots contain more sugar than any other vegetable.**

Method
Butter the bread if desired and leave aside. Chop the spring onions and tomatoes. Rip the lettuce with your hands so that you have enough to fill two cups. Ripping the lettuce prevents bruising to the leaves. Cool the boiled eggs in cold water and peel off the shells. If you have an egg slicer, use this; otherwise, chop the egg with a sharp knife. Mix all these together in a bowl. Add the cheese. Wash and peel the carrot and grate it into the mixture. Add the mayonnaise. If there is mixture left over, it will last over night in the fridge. Season with salt and pepper. Spread onto four slices of bread and place the other four slices on top. Cut into triangles. Delicious.

chicken caesar pitta

Makes ❹

Ingredients

2 chicken breasts
pepper and salt
1 dessertspoon olive oil
4 slices pancetta (streaky rashers)
4 pitta bread pockets
cos lettuce

Caesar dressing

1 egg
$^1/_2$ teaspoon Worcestershire sauce
$^1/_2$ teaspoon Dijon mustard
1 tablespoon lime juice
1 dessertspoon Parmesan cheese, grated
$^1/_2$ clove garlic, crushed
$^3/_4$ cup olive oil
seasoning

Method

Wash and dry the chicken and dust with pepper and salt. Add olive oil to a pan and fry the chicken on medium heat for about 10 minutes each side. Remove to a plate and allow to cool. Wipe out the pan with some kitchen paper and put another drop of oil into it. Fry the pancetta until crispy on both sides, then drain on kitchen paper.

Method for dressing

Place the egg in a food processor. Add all the dressing ingredients except the oil and seasoning. Blast for thirty seconds with the lid ON. Season. Remove the lid-plug and turn on the processor. Slowly add the olive oil continuously until the sound of the mixer changes as the dressing starts to thicken. Don't make it too thick—just a coating consistency.

Open the 4 pitta pockets and tear in the lettuce. Cut the chicken into strips and pop it into the pitta. Add the dressing and finally the bacon.

If you want to make it extra crunchy, add some croutons. For homemade croutons, see page 196.

char-grilled chicken on herb bread

Makes 4 rounds of sandwiches

Ingredients
2 tablespoons vegetable oil
2 teaspoons soy sauce
1 teaspoon honey
2 chicken breasts
8 slices herb bread
2 handfuls of salad leaves
8 green grapes
$^1/_2$ cup mayonnaise
1 dessertspoon fresh pesto
to serve: **tortilla chips or extra salad leaves**

> Bees may travel as far as 80,000 km and visit more than two million flowers to gather enough nectar to make just a pound of honey. Hard work.

Method
Mix the oil, soy sauce and honey together in a bowl. Place the chicken in this mixture and puncture the flesh with a fork. Cover with cling film and chill in the fridge for 2 hours.

Place mayonnaise in a bowl and add fresh pesto. If you have a griddle pan, use this; otherwise, a normal frying pan will do. Char-grill the chicken on a medium heat for about 8 minutes each side or until cooked through. Cool and cut each breast in half, lengthways. Take four slices of the bread and put half a breast on each slice, followed by some salad leaves. Cut the grapes in half and pop on top of the leaves. Add a dessertspoon of the pesto mayonnaise to each slice. Now put on the top slices of bread and serve on a plate with some tortilla chips or some extra salad leaves. Just heavenly!

sausage strolls

Serves **4**

Ingredients
150 g (5 oz) plain flour
pinch of salt
75 g (3 oz) hard margarine
cold water
400 g (14 oz) fresh sausage meat
some beaten egg

Method
Sieve the flour and salt into a bowl. Slice in the margarine with a knife, then rub it in using the tips of your fingers, until the mixture looks like fine breadcrumbs. Trickle in enough of the cold water to mix to a stiff paste. Sprinkle some flour onto your kitchen counter or a clean surface. Roll out the pastry into a square shape, trimming the edges with a knife. Place the sausage meat onto the middle of the pastry, and roll into a cylindrical shape. Wet the edge of the pastry to seal the roll shut. Cut into 8 cm ($3^{1}/_{4}$ in) pieces and place on a greased baking tray. Make a slit on the top of each one and rub with beaten egg. Cook in a hot oven (170°C/350°F/gas mark 7) for 5 minutes, then reduce the heat to 160°C (315°F/gas mark 6) for a further 10 minutes.

Alternatively, you can use a packet of bought frozen puff pastry. Just defrost and proceed as above. Enjoy!

homemade hamburgers with potato wedges

Makes ❹

Ingredients

Hamburgers

500 g (18 oz) round steak, minced
1 tablespoon chopped onion
1 clove garlic (crushed or creamed)
seasoning—pepper and salt
dash of soy sauce or Worcestershire sauce
1 tablespoon chopped parsley
1 teaspoon Italian seasoning
1 beaten egg (optional)

for frying: **olive oil**

Potato wedges
1 medium potato for every 8 wedges
olive oil
Italian seasoning
seasoning—pepper and salt
to serve: **4 warm baps and relish or dressing of your choice**

Method

Place all the hamburger ingredients in a bowl and mix well. Dip your hands into cold water and then divide the mixture into four. Press out gently into circles and smooth down. Heat a little olive oil in a frying pan, allowing it to get hot. Now add the hamburgers and fry for 1 minute. Then turn them over and lower the heat and continue to cook them until juices run clear. Drain them on kitchen paper and serve on warm baps with relish or dressing of your choice.

Method for potato wedges

First wash and dry the potatoes, but do not peel them. Cut into wedges—you should get about eight per potato. Rub over with olive oil, then sprinkle with Italian seasoning and salt and pepper. Place on a baking tray and bake in a moderate oven (140°–160°C/ 275°–315°F/gas mark 4–5) for approximately 20 minutes or until golden brown.

tikka masala wrap

Makes **4**

Ingredients
2 chicken breasts
1 tablespoon of vegetable oil
2 tablespoons tikka masala cooking sauce (from shop)
1 cup shredded lettuce
2 tablespoons mayonnaise
2 teaspoons mango chutney
4 soft flour tortillas or 4 small nan breads
to serve: **raita (see page 74) or red onion marmalade (see page 57), if desired**

Method
Wash and dry the chicken. Slice each breast in two, lengthways. Heat the oil in a frying pan on a medium heat and fry the chicken until golden brown. Add the tikka masala sauce and stir well. Bring to the boil, then lower the heat and cover the pan. Let simmer for 6–7 minutes. Remove from heat and allow to cool in the sauce. Add the lettuce, mayonnaise and mango chutney.

To make up the wrap, divide the mixture between the four tortillas. Roll up and cut in two at a slant. Serve a little raita or red onion marmalade on the side, if you like. A bit different.

cool hot dog

Makes ❹

Ingredients

4 frankfurters
4 dessertspoons finely chopped onion
4 dessertspoons chopped tomato
2 slices ham
4 soft bread rolls
American mustard
tomato ketchup
2 sliced pickles (optional)

Method

Place the frankfurters in boiling water in a saucepan and cook for 5 minutes. Chop the onion on a chopping board (see page 25 for how to chop onions). Slice the tomato and ham. Pop a cooked frankfurter into each roll and cover with strips of the ham. Add the onion and tomato. Squirt in the mustard and ketchup to taste. Add the pickles, if desired. So easy and it's the dogs!

John Montague
(1718–1792) was the
fourth Earl of Sandwich.
A serious gambler, he
would order his servant
to bring him meat tucked
in between bread. Others
began to order 'the same
as Sandwich!' The
original sandwich was, in
fact, a piece of salt beef
between two slices of
toasted bread. Yuck!

the ultimate club

Makes **4**

Ingredients

8 rashers

6 leaves of lettuce

3 medium tomatoes

8 slices of cooked smoked chicken or
turkey

12 slices of bread

mayonnaise

2 slices of Swiss cheese

8 cocktail sticks

Method

Grill the rashers on both sides until crispy. Allow to cool. Wash and dry the lettuce and
slice up the tomatoes. You can buy cooked sliced chicken breast in a pack at any good
supermarket or you can use turkey slices from your local deli. Toast the bread and spread
mayonnaise on each slice. Now you get to build your masterpiece.

On layer one, place the lettuce, chicken and tomato, then put on the second slice of toast, and
build up with the bacon and cheese. Add the top piece of toast. Secure each half sandwich with
a cocktail stick. Now you can cut your club in two. Remove the sticks before you chow down.

smoothies

Peanut butter contains a minimum of 90 per cent peanuts. The spread was first sold on store shelves in 1908 in California in the USA.

yellow nutter

Serves ❷

Bananas are full of potassium and there is enough calcium in the rest to be a bone idol!

Ingredients
2 fresh bananas, sliced
3 scoops banana ice-cream
2 dessertspoons peanut butter
200 ml (7 fl oz) milk

Method
Place all the ingredients in the blender and give it a whiz until your required smoothness is reached.

minted and mellow

Serves ❷

This smoothie is very refreshing with a little zest from the lime to kick your taste buds into action.

Ingredients
1 medium honeydew melon or 3 cups diced melon (if pre-packed)
$^1/_2$ teaspoon fresh ginger, grated
2 tablespoons fresh lime juice
2 dessertspoons chopped fresh mint
8 ice cubes
100 ml (4 fl oz) 7up or sprite
1 teaspoon sugar
to serve: 2 slices of lime

Method
Slice the melon in half and scoop out the seeds. Cut out as much flesh as you can and put it in the blender. Peel and grate the fresh ginger. Cut the lime in two and squeeze enough juice to fill 1 tablespoon. Chop up the mint and add this, along with the ginger and lime juice, to the blender. More lime juice can be added to taste. Pop in the ice and blend for 10 seconds. Add the 7up and sugar until enough smoothness is reached. Pour into two tall glasses and garnish with a slice of lime.

bloody berry

Serves ❷

This one is packed with vitamin C to keep your nose out of trouble.

Ingredients
1¹/₂ cups fresh strawberries
1 cup fresh or frozen raspberries
100 ml (4 fl oz) cranberry juice
1 strawberry yoghurt (average size)
50 ml (2 fl oz) milk

Method
Wash and dry the strawberries and raspberries in a colander. Remove the green stalks from the strawberries. Pop the berries in a blender with the rest of the ingredients and blast for 20 seconds. Pour into 2 glasses and sip with a straw. Seriously tasty.

raspberry daze

Simple but mind-numbingly tasty!

Serves ❹

> Raspberries contain a natural substance called ellagic acid, which is an anti-carcinogenic (cancer-preventing) compound.

Ingredients
3 cups frozen raspberries
200 ml (7 fl oz) freshly squeezed orange juice (You can buy a bottle of freshly squeezed pure orange juice at your local supermarket. If you can't find a bottle of pure juice, get squeezing, as there is no substitute for the real thing in this case.)

Method
Place ingredients in blender and bash around for 20 seconds. This is a great cold buster.

kiwi king

Serves **4**

Ingredients

2 limes
200 ml (7 fl oz) cranberry juice
tip of a teaspoon of freshly grated ginger
8 ice cubes
3 kiwis

> Kiwis contain vitamins E and A. They are a good source of anti-oxidants and dietary fibre. A kiwi contains as much vitamin C as an orange.

Method

Cut the limes in half and squeeze them. Pour the lime into the blender with the cranberry juice. Pop in the ginger followed by the ice and blend until all the ice is crushed. Scoop the kiwi flesh into a sieve and mash it through the sieve with a fork into a bowl. This prevents the seeds from being crushed in the blender which creates a bitter taste. Stir the strained kiwi into the rest of the smoothie.

pina co-ladmad

Serves **4**

Ingredients

1 cup light coconut milk
2 scoops vanilla ice-cream
1 cup pineapple cubes (drain the tinned ones if fresh pineapple is not available)
1 tablespoon lemon juice
4 cubes of ice

> Coconut milk, when refrigerated, separates naturally. The cream goes to the top.
>
> Indians used pineapple leaves to make fences. The leaves are very sharp and worked as protection.

Method

Place all the ingredients in the blender and blitz until well mixed.

Apples are 80 per cent water and 20 per cent air—that's why they float.

strapps

Serves **4**

Ingredients
8 plump strawberries
200 ml (7 fl oz) apple juice
10 ice cubes

Method
Wash the strawberries and cut off the stalks. Pop them in the blender with the apple juice and ice. Blast until all the ice is crushed.

This tastes so good, you'd think it should be bad for you—but it's good in every way!

new england lemonade

Ingredients
300 ml (11 fl oz) freshly squeezed lemon juice (approximately 7–8 medium lemons—when selecting them, remember that the smooth-skinned ones give more juice as they have less rind and more flesh)
700 ml (1¹/₄ pt) cold water
to serve: **slices of lemon, if desired**

Sugar water
¹/₂ cup sugar
3 tablespoons boiling water

Method
Squeeze the lemon juice from the lemons. Put the lemon juice and the cold water into a jug for serving. If desired, add some lemon slices for appearance. In a small cup or bowl, mix the sugar and the boiling water. Stir well, then heat in the microwave until all of the sugar has been dissolved. Put into a smaller jug and serve with the lemonade, allowing each person to sweeten to their taste. Serve in glasses filled up with ice cubes. This is a great thirst quencher on a hot day!

dvds

stuffed green peppers with ratatouille

Serves **4**

Ingredients
4 green peppers
olive oil for rubbing over pepper
1 courgette
1 aubergine (optional)
1 yellow pepper
1 red pepper
4 medium tomatoes
1 red onion
1 clove garlic (creamed)
1 tablespoon olive oil
2 teaspoons tomato purée
seasoning—salt and pepper
to garnish: basil leaves

Method
Place the green peppers on a chopping board and cut in half lengthways. Cut around stalks, remove and shake out seeds. Rub all over with olive oil, then place on a baking tray and bake in oven at 160°C (350°F/gas mark 4) for approximately 8 minutes. Remove and allow to cool.

Method for Ratatouille
Wash and slice the courgette. Wash the aubergine and cut it in half, then into slices. Cut these slices into small cubes. Cut the red and yellow peppers in half and remove the seeds and stalks. Cut into slices, then into cubes. Cut the tomatoes into quarters. Peel and slice the onion. Cream the garlic (see page 19). Heat the oil in a saucepan or casserole dish. Add the courgette, pepper, onion and aubergine, and cook for 5 minutes with the lid on. Remove the lid and add the tomatoes, tomato purée, seasoning and garlic. Cook with the lid on for 5 minutes. Tear in some basil leaves. Now spoon some mixture into each pepper. Place on a baking tray and reheat in oven until hot. Serve on a plate with whole fresh basil leaves placed around the base.

spanish omelette

Serves **4**

Ingredients
4 medium potatoes
1 small onion
2 tablespoons olive oil, for frying
2 medium eggs
seasoning
1 clove garlic, crushed

Method
Wash, peel and slice the potatoes. Peel and chop the onion (see page 25). Heat the oil in a frying pan, then sauté the potatoes on a medium heat for a few minutes, turning while cooking. Add the onion and garlic and continue to sauté until slightly soft. Place on kitchen paper on a plate.

In a bowl, beat the eggs with pepper and salt. Add crushed garlic, onion and potatoes and mash into the eggs with a fork until a firm mixture is achieved.

Heat a dessertspoon of olive oil in a small frying pan. Add the egg mixture and cook for 8–10 minutes on a low to medium heat or until slightly set.

Turn out carefully onto a plate. Do this by placing the plate upside down on top of the pan and turning both together. Slip back into frying pan, uncooked side down, and continue to cook until set. Turn out onto a serving plate. Cut into wedges and serve on its own or with salad leaves.

Alternatively the mixture can be placed in the frying pan to start on top of the cooker and then finished off in the oven at a moderate temperature.

gambas pil-pil (prawns in garlic olive oil)

Serves **4**

Here's a recipe for the cheating vegetarians out there who can't say no to a bit of fish now and then! For this dish, use the best prawns you can afford. The Dublin Bay prawns can be used with shells either on or removed. The Pacific prawn shells are black before cooking but turn a lovely light tan colour when cooked. This dish is cooked very quickly and should be served straightaway.

Ingredients
2 tablespoons olive oil
2 cloves garlic, crushed
$^1/_4$ teaspoon chopped red chilli (optional)
100 g (4 oz) Dublin Bay prawns, tails on OR 100 g (4 oz) Pacific (tiger) prawns OR
  100 g (4 oz) defrosted prawns

Method
Heat olive oil in a frying pan. Add crushed garlic and chilli and cook for 1 minute. Add prawns and toss well in oil for approx 5 minutes for uncooked prawns or 3 minutes for already-cooked prawns. Turn out into small serving dishes. Serve with garlic bread or French stick. Be careful cooking this dish as it gets very hot. This is a traditional Spanish dish and is served in Spain in all the tapas bars.

garlic mushrooms (two ways!)

Serves **4**

There are two ways of doing this lovely dish

Ingredients 1
100 g (4 oz) button mushrooms or medium-
 sized mushrooms
1 small plate flour
1 small plate beaten eggs
1 small plate fine breadcrumbs

Garlic Butter
1 cm ($^1/_2$ in) slice fresh butter
$^1/_2$ clove garlic, crushed

Method 1
Wash and dry the mushrooms. Dip each
mushroom first in flour, then in egg, and
finally in breadcrumbs. Deep fry for a few
minutes until golden. Drain on kitchen
paper. Serve with garlic butter.

Method for garlic butter
Add the garlic to the butter and mash
together with a fork. Melt in microwave for
15 seconds.

Ingredients 2
100 g (4 oz) medium mushrooms
2 tablespoons olive oil
2 cloves garlic, crushed
1 dessertspoon chopped parsley

Method 2
Wash, dry and slice mushrooms. Heat the
olive oil in a frying pan. Add the garlic,
mushrooms and parsley and cook for 2
minutes. Remove to plate with kitchen
paper.

Serve with Melba toast (page 40) or a
rustic crunchy bread of your choice.

tomato salsa and tortilla chips

Serves ❹

This salsa will put a zing to your thing.

Ingredients
6 large ripe tomatoes
¹/₂ small onion
juice of 1 lime
1 clove of garlic, crushed
1 small red or green chilli
salt and pepper
¹/₂ cup of fresh coriander
tortilla chips

Method
Dice up the tomatoes and finely slice the onion. Place in a bowl. Add the lime juice and garlic. Cut off the chilli stalk and slice the chilli lengthways first. Then chop it up as small as you can. Make sure you don't rub your eyes or face. Put the chilli in the bowl and wash your hands straightaway. Add salt and pepper and the coriander leaves. Stir together well. Take half the salsa and pop it into the liquidiser for 30 seconds. Pour back into the bowl and stir into the chunkier half. Chill for 1 hour before serving.

If you want to impress your friends with your skills, you can make your own tortilla chips. You will need 4 tortillas and a deep-fat fryer. Cut the tortillas into triangle sections as if dividing up a pizza. Throw them in the fryer at full heat until crisp. Drain on kitchen paper.

black-eyed beans with chestnut mushroom and thai green sauce

Serves 4

Ingredients
1 cup black-eyed beans
6 chestnut (brown) mushrooms
1 tablespoon vegetable oil
1 clove garlic
1 tablespoon Thai green curry sauce
seasoning—salt and pepper

Method
Black-eyed beans are easily available at health-food stores or in some supermarkets. Place beans in a bowl, cover with boiling water and allow to soak for half an hour. Place in a saucepan, making sure that they are covered with water. Bring to the boil, lower heat and simmer for about 15 minutes or until soft. Strain off the water but keep some liquid aside. Wash and dry the mushrooms and cut into quarters. Heat the oil in a saucepan. Add the mushrooms and sauté for 5 minutes. Crush in the garlic and cook for 1 minute. Remove to plate. Place a little extra oil in the saucepan, and heat gently. Add Thai curry sauce and cook for 1 minute. Add beans, and stir well. Add mushrooms, garlic and seasoning. If mixture looks too dry at this stage, add some of the water which you put aside after cooking the beans. Bring to the boil and serve. This dish doesn't look great but it tastes amazing. Place in a bowl and serve with chips or ciabatta.

veggie paella

Serves **4**

Ingredients
1 courgette (sliced)
1 red pepper
1 yellow pepper
8 mangetouts
4 baby sweet corn
4 asparagus tips
1 tablespoon olive oil
1 clove garlic (crushed)
1 cup long-grain rice
$^1/_4$ teaspoon powdered saffron or 6 strands
1 cup vegetable stock or water
pepper and salt
1 lemon
fresh coriander

Method
Wash the courgette and slice it using a sharp knife. Cut the peppers in half, lengthways, and remove the seeds and green stalk. Cut into strips about 1 cm ($^1/_2$ in) wide, and then into squares. Cut mangetouts in half and baby corn into thirds. Leave the asparagus tips whole. Heat the oil in a frying pan and add the veggies except for the asparagus. Cook on a low heat for about 5 minutes. Add garlic and asparagus tips and cook for 2 minutes. Put the rice in a sieve and wash it. Shake off the water and pop it in the frying pan. Continue to cook for 3 more minutes. Add the saffron and stock and bring to the boil. Season. Cover and allow to simmer for 15 minutes or until rice is *aldente*. Serve in a big bowl with wedges of lemon and fresh coriander leaves on top. When serving, make sure that each person adds a good squeeze of lemon. Gorgeous.

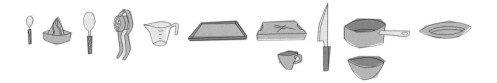

aubergine and mushroom kebabs with peanut butter sauce

Serves ❹

Ingredients

2 aubergines, cut in 3 cm (1¹/₄ in) pieces
150 g (5 oz) chestnut mushrooms or
  button mushrooms

Marinade

1 teaspoon ground cumin
1 teaspoon ground coriander
3 cm (1¹/₄ in) piece of root ginger, peeled
and finely chopped
2 cloves garlic, crushed
2 tablespoons lemon juice
1 stalk lemon grass
4 tablespoons sunflower oil

Peanut Butter Sauce

¹/₂ teaspoon ground cumin
¹/₂ teaspoon ground coriander
1 clove garlic, crushed
1 small onion, chopped
1 tablespoon lime juice
¹/₂ red chilli, de-seeded and chopped
125 ml (4¹/₂ fl oz) coconut milk
1 cup crunchy peanut butter
140 ml (5 fl oz) cold water

Method

Thread the cut aubergine and clean mushrooms onto skewers. Place all the marinade ingredients in a jug or bowl and mix well. Place the skewers on a plate and spoon the marinade over. Leave for 2 hours.

Place on a baking tray and brush again with marinade. Cook for 10–15 minutes in a moderate oven (140°–160°C/275°–315°F/gas mark 4–5). Place on a serving dish and serve the sauce separately.

Method for sauce

Place all the ingredients in a small saucepan. Bring to the boil, stirring all the time. Simmer until sauce is the required thickness—not too thick and not too thin.

hummus and veggie chips

Serves **2**

This recipe for hummus is delicious and so easy. Great for a healthy snack while watching your favourite movie.

Ingredients
1 teaspoon toasted sesame seeds
1 cup chickpeas (we use the tinned ones)
2 dessertspoons lemon juice
1 dessertspoon chopped fresh basil
1 clove garlic, crushed
2 dessertspoons crème fraîche
pepper and salt

Veggie chips
2 carrots
1 parsnip
1 large potato
olive oil

Method
To toast the sesame seeds, pop them in a dry non-stick pan and heat over a medium heat for a minute, tossing them a few times. You might hear them pop. This is normal. Open the tin of chickpeas and drain the juice off into a cup. Put the liquid aside. Place chickpeas, sesame seeds, lemon juice, basil and crushed garlic in the liquidiser or processor and blast for 30 seconds. Add the crème fraîche, pepper and salt and 1 dessertspoon of the liquid left over from draining the chickpeas. Blend until smooth. Scrape out into a bowl and chill until required.

Method for veggie chips
Wash and peel the vegetables. Slice the carrot and parsnip lengthways into thin strips. First, take off the head and cut them in half lengthways, then run the knife through each half, as many times as you can. Slice the potato thinly. Using a pastry brush, brush all the vegetables with a light coating of olive oil. Place them on a baking tray and bake in a medium to high oven until crisp.

posh pitta stir-fry

Serves ❹

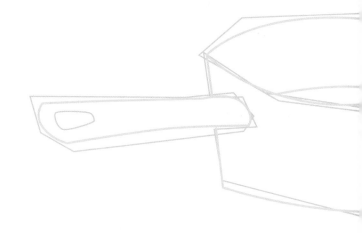

Ingredients
1 sheet medium noodles
8 mangetouts
4 tomatoes
¹/₄ of a cucumber
1 small red onion
1 tablespoon vegetable oil
1 cup bean sprouts
4 pitta breads

Pesto Mayonnaise
1 teaspoon pesto
¹/₂ cup mayonnaise

Method
Soak noodles in boiling water for 10 minutes. Drain and set aside.

Prepare all the vegetables and cut the tomatoes, cucumber and onion in slices. Heat the oil in a wok or frying pan. Add the vegetables and toss for about 3 minutes. Add bean sprouts and toss for 1 minute. Heat pitta breads under grill until warmed. Fill cavity of each with stir-fry. Serve pesto mayonnaise separately or add some to the vegetables before filling into pitta.

Method for pesto mayonnaise
Add the pesto to the mayonnaise and mix well.

soups

In all our soup recipes, we use freshly ground black pepper and homemade chicken stock.

There are hundreds of soups out there, ready to be created. We have narrowed it down to our top five faves for you to enjoy, but be careful when liquidising the hot liquids—a soup wand might be a better option for smaller chefs.

CHICKEN STOCK

Place chicken parts in a saucepan and cover with cold water. Add a pinch of mixed herbs or some fresh thyme and a carrot. Cover and simmer for 30 minutes. Strain into a bowl and discard the non-liquid.

Raspberry sorbet

Carrot cake

Chocolate mousse

Chocolate chip
shortbread cookies

Danish strawberry shortcake

Fruity cous cous

Wild rice, red pepper and prawn salad

Caesar salad

Red cabbage salad with pistachio nuts

sweet red pepper soup

Serves ❹

Ingredients
2 medium potatoes
1 long pointed red pepper
1 medium onion
1 tablespoon olive oil
1 clove garlic
1 litre (1³/₄ pt) chicken stock
pepper and salt to taste

Method
Peel and chop the potatoes. Cut open the pepper and take out the seeds. Peel the onion and cut into quarters. Pour olive oil into a saucepan and allow to warm up. Crush in the garlic and add the veggies, stirring for a few minutes. Pour in the stock and season. Bring to the boil, then simmer for 20 minutes or until veggies are soft. Liquidise when cooked or hand mash for a chunkier texture. Serve hot.

curried parsnip & apple soup

Serves ❹

Ingredients
2 small parsnips
1 medium cooking apple
2 medium potatoes
1 onion
1 tablespoon vegetable oil
1 clove garlic
1 heaped teaspoon of curry powder
1 litre (1³/₄ pt) chicken stock
pepper and salt

Method
Peel the parsnips, apples, potatoes and onion. Chop and put aside. Heat the oil in a large saucepan and crush in the garlic. Add the prepared veggies straight away and stir for a few minutes. Throw in the curry powder and mix well until all the veggies are coated. Pour in the chicken stock and season. Simmer for 30 minutes. Liquidise and serve.

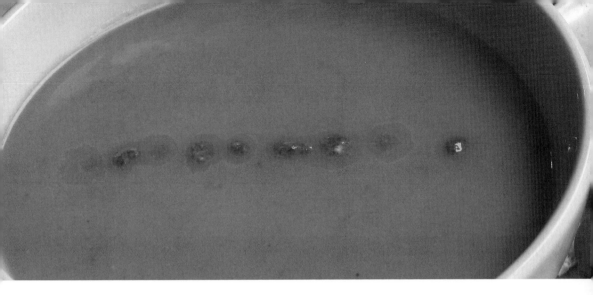

carrot & coriander soup

Serves ❹

Ingredients
3 medium carrots
1 onion
2 medium potatoes
1 tablespoon vegetable oil
1 clove garlic
1 teaspoon ground coriander
1 litre (1³/₄ pt) chicken stock
salt and pepper
1 handful freshly chopped coriander

Method
Peel and chop all the vegetables. Heat the oil in a large saucepan and crush in the garlic.
Add vegetables straightaway and stir on a medium heat for a few minutes. Sprinkle in the
ground coriander and add the stock. Season and bring to the boil. Simmer for 30 minutes.
Liquidise, then taste for flavour. Add chopped coriander and serve.

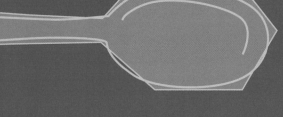

chorizo &
white bean soup

Serves **4**

Ingredients
4 medium tomatoes
1 onion
2 tablespoons olive oil
2 cloves garlic, crushed
1 cup chopped chorizo sausage
1 cup mixed cubed peppers
1 teaspoon chopped red chillies
1 litre (1^3/$_4$ pt) chicken stock
^{1}/$_2$ cup pasta shells
1 cup tinned butter beans, drained
pepper and salt

Method
Chop up the tomatoes and put aside. Next, chop the onion. Heat some olive oil in a saucepan to a sizzling temperature. Sauté the garlic and onion for a few minutes. Add the chopped chorizo and fry for approximately 2 minutes. Add the peppers and chopped tomatoes and chillies. Stir well. Pour in the stock and bring to the boil. Add the pasta and simmer for 10 minutes. Pop in the white beans, and simmer for 5 minutes. Season and serve.

celeriac &
pine nut soup

Serves ❹

Ingredients
100 g (4 oz) peeled, chopped celeriac
2 medium potatoes
1 onion, chopped
1 tablespoon vegetable oil
1 tablespoon pine nuts
1 clove garlic, crushed
³/₄ litre (1¹/₄ pt) chicken stock
bouquet garni, (mixture of thyme, parsley and bay leaf)
pepper and salt
to garnish: **chopped parsley**

Method
Prepare all the vegetables first. Peel and chop the celeriac—this is a hard vegetable so cut it into quarters to make it easier to peel. Wash the potatoes and peel and chop them also. Peel and chop the onion (see page 25).

Pour the oil into the saucepan and fry the pine nuts until golden. Add the onion, celeriac and garlic, and sauté for a few minutes. Pour in the stock and pop in the bouquet garni (if you don't have one, just add a small pinch of the herbs mentioned). Bring to the boil and add the potatoes and salt and pepper. Simmer for 20 minutes or until the vegetables are soft. Liquidise. Taste and adjust seasoning. Serve with a little chopped parsley on top. A great winter warmer!

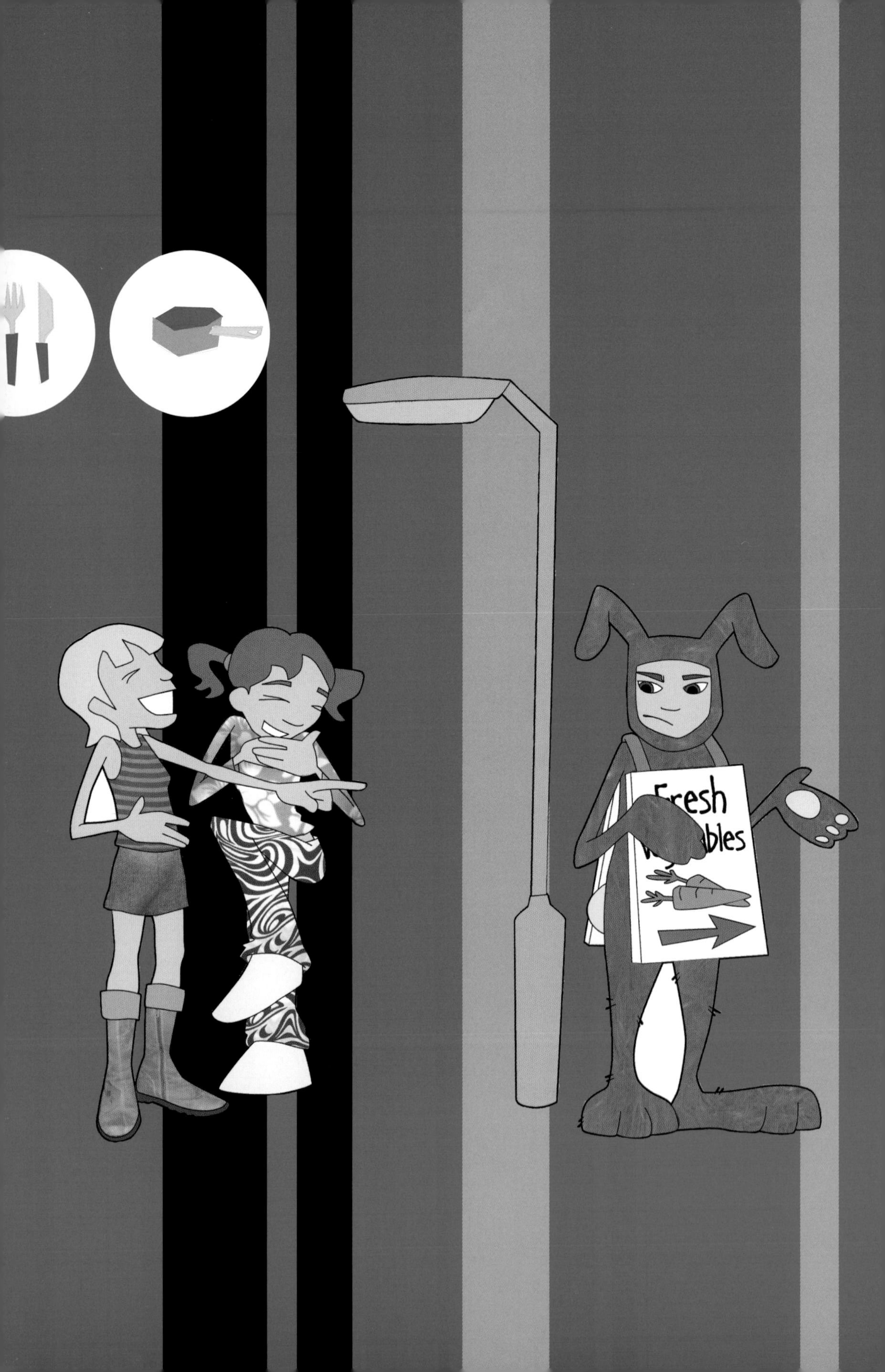

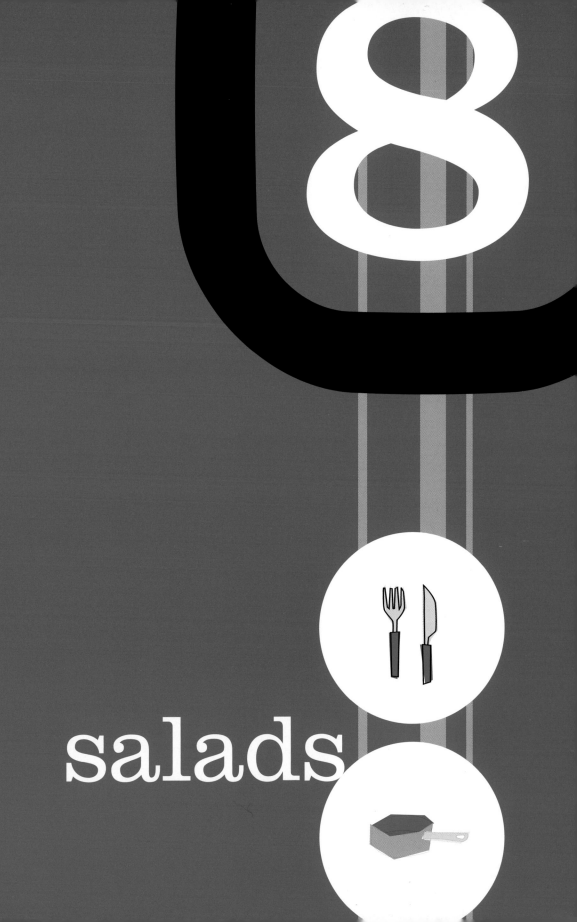

181

salads

Lettuce alone

There are numerous leafy greens out there in the deep shelves of pre-packed salads. We are covering a few leaves for your heads!

It is a better idea to use lettuce bought loose—the pre-packed ones are often washed in a chlorine solution and the bags are treated to hold freshness. Handy but not as good as the real thing.

Preparing lettuce

Before serving, rinse the lettuce in a colander, using cold water. Shake off the excess water and pat dry with some kitchen tissue or a towel. If your leaves are looking a bit flat, try putting them in ice-cold water for a few seconds. Salad dressing will cling to dry lettuce only; if the lettuce is wet, all the dressing will remain at the bottom of the bowl.

Always tear lettuce leaves by hand — this prevents damage. Cutting them will release an oxide that destroys the vitamin C content. However, iceberg lettuce can be cut.

Because lettuce is mostly water, it does not store for a long period of time. Do not store your lettuce with fruit. Some fruits contain a natural ripening gas that can cause lettuce to decay. Special thanks to Mary Ferriter of Ballyferriter— a bit of a lettuce guru.

Butterhead Lettuce

This comes in a round loose head of leaves with a smooth buttery texture. It has a mild flavour and works well in sandwiches. Not the most exciting leaf for a sassy salad. Butterhead is the Mona Lisa of lettuce—very famous but plain to look at.

Iceberg

This comes in a firm round head and can be sliced with a sharp knife. Iceberg is mostly used for garnishes. Ideal in a burger, it's very crisp and lasts longer than most lettuces. Iceberg is one of the most chemically treated lettuces, so make sure you buy organic.

Romaine

This lettuce comes in a long head with sturdy leaves. It is also known as cos lettuce. Romaine lettuce has been around since Roman times and is the one and only lettuce to be used in a proper Caesar salad. It has a nice strong flavour and a crisp bite.

Lollo Rosso

A showy leaf that looks great in a mixed salad. This lettuce has frilly leaves and varies in colour. At the stalk it starts off green, turning a deep red at the top.

Oak Leaf

A curvy purple lettuce with a slightly bitter flavour, it works great with mixed greens as a visual contrast and different taste.

Lamb's (tongue) Lettuce

Also known as corn salad, this has a lovely delicate flavour. It is a little rounded leaf, and you will find it in most pre-packed salads. Good things do come in small packages.

Frisee

The punk rocker of lettuce, frisee is spiky and ragged in appearance. The ends of the leaves are dark green, fading to lightest greeny yellow in the centre. It has a bitter sharp taste. Goes well with a no-nonsense dressing

Sorrel

Sorrel has long pointy leaves that are rounded off at the top. It has a sharp taste. Mix it with milder leaves to complement its flavour.

Radicchio

This is a great salad lettuce. It has looks and taste. With deep-red leafs in a tight head, radicchio has a peppery flavour. It can also be sautéed or used like a wrap.

Rocket

This is a great addition to salads. A herb in its own right, rocket has enjoyed the limelight in top restaurants on salads and in sauces. Now that it's more readily available in most supermarkets, you can bring the bistro to your home. Rocket has a hot peppery taste. Would you believe it was originally a weed?

Baby Spinach

Dark green and delicate in appearance, baby spinach is not classically a lettuce, but it is used in most modern salads. It is rich in fibre and anti-oxidants.

Mary Ferriter's lettuce garden in the heart of Kerry

red ripe berry salad

Serves ❹

Ingredients
1 punnet fresh raspberries
¹/₂ punnet red currants
¹/₂ punnet strawberries
a large colander full of mixed salad leaves
2 dessertspoons sesame seeds
50 g (2 oz) goat's cheese (optional)

Dressing
1 tablespoon raspberry vinegar
3 tablespoons olive oil
pepper and salt
¹/₂ teaspoon Dijon mustard
¹/₂ teaspoon honey
¹/₄ teaspoon crushed garlic

Method
Wash and dry all the berries. Destalk the strawberries and red currants. Place all the dry lettuce in a large decorative salad bowl. Add the berries and sesame seeds. Fold the berries through the leaves with your hands so you don't crush them. Sprinkle the dressing all around the salad. This is a truly scrumptious salad. The mix of sweetness and tart is sensational.

Method for dressing
Put it all together in a screw-top jar and shake it all about.

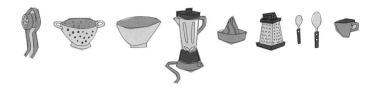

caesar salad

Serves **4**

Ingredients
1 head romaine (or cos) lettuce
1 egg
$^1/_2$ clove garlic, crushed
dash of Worcestershire sauce
juice of $^1/_2$ lime
$^1/_4$ teaspoon dry mustard or Dijon mustard
seasoning—pepper and salt
1 dessertspoon freshly grated Parmesan cheese
$^1/_2$ cup olive oil
1 or 2 tinned anchovies (optional)
to finish: croutons and light shavings of Parmesan cheese

Method
A true Caesar salad is made with romaine or cos lettuce. Wash and dry the lettuce and place in a salad bowl.

For the dressing, crack the egg into a blender and add the garlic and Worcestershire sauce. Blend for a few seconds, then add the lime juice, mustard, seasoning and Parmesan cheese. Blend again for a few seconds, then turn the blender to the lowest setting and slowly add the olive oil, blending all the time, until required thickness is reached—it should be a light thickness. Pour the dressing over the lettuce and add the anchovies (if using), croutons and some light shavings of Parmesan cheese. Cooked chicken and prawns are optional, but we prefer it on its own. See page 196 for fresh croutons.

festival chicken salad

Serves **4**

This is one of the favourite recipes throughout all the years. Double or triple the ingredients and make a big bowl to bring to barbecues or parties and you will have everyone asking for the recipe!

Ingredients
4 cooked chicken breasts
herbs—parsley and tarragon
seasoning—salt and pepper
1 mango or 1 tin peaches in light syrup
1 tablespoon sultanas
1 teaspoon lemon juice
3 tablespoons mayonnaise
seasoning—black pepper and salt
1 tablespoon mango chutney
$^1/_2$ teaspoon mild curry powder
1 tablespoon toasted cashew nuts

Method
To cook the chicken, place it in a saucepan with enough cold water to cover it. Add herbs and seasoning, bring to the boil and simmer for 30 minutes. Drain and cool.

Place the chicken on a chopping board and cut into cubes. Put the cubes in a bowl. Peel and slice the mango, leaving behind the grisly centre stone, then cut the flesh into cubes. Add to the chicken. Now add the sultanas, lemon juice, mayonnaise, seasoning, mango chutney and curry powder. Sprinkle in half the cashew nuts. Mix well. Pour into a nice serving bowl. Garnish with the remaining nuts. Serve with crispy salad leaves and fresh bread.

fillet steak and beetroot salad with horseradish and balsamic dressing

Serves ❹

Ingredients
100 g (4 oz) fillet steak in one piece
a little olive oil, for rubbing over steak
pepper and salt
1 tablespoon olive oil, for frying
1 packet washed mixed salad leaves
4 small baby beetroots
4 slices of beetroot

Dressing
3 tablespoons olive oil
$^{1}/_{2}$ teaspoon crushed clove of garlic
$^{1}/_{4}$ teaspoon creamed horseradish sauce
$^{1}/_{4}$ teaspoon grain mustard
1 tablespoon balsamic vinegar
pepper and salt

Method
Rub the steak with a little olive oil and dust with black pepper. Heat 1 tablespoon of olive oil in a frying pan and seal all sides of the steak. Turn down the heat and continue to cook until required doneness is reached (approximately 5 minutes for rare or 15 minutes for well done). Remove to plate and allow to cool. Arrange lettuce on a large serving dish. Place beetroot to one side of dish. Slice filet steak and arrange on lettuce. Pour dressing over or serve separately.

Method for dressing
Place 1 tablespoon of olive oil in a small saucepan. Add the garlic and cook for 30 seconds. Add horseradish sauce and grain mustard. Add balsamic vinegar and the rest of the olive oil. Allow to heat through. Season. Serve hot or cold.

red cabbage salad with pistachio nuts

Serves **4**

Ingredients
2 cups red cabbage (shredded)
$^1/_2$ cup balsamic vinegar
1 dessertspoon sugar
$^3/_4$ cup pistachio nuts (shells removed)
pepper and salt
1 cup olive oil

Method
To shred the red cabbage, place it on a chopping board and cut into thin slices with a sharp knife.

Place the shredded cabbage in a bowl. Put the vinegar and sugar in a saucepan and heat to boiling point. Pour over the cabbage and toss well. Just watch the colour of the cabbage becoming shiny and bright. Allow to cool. Add the pistachio nuts and seasoning. Pour on the olive oil and mix through. Chill until required.

mixed bean with mint and honey dressing

Serves ❹

Ingredients
1 cup mixed beans
salt and pepper to season

Dressing
1 dessertspoon chopped mint
1 tablespoon white wine vinegar
1 teaspoon honey
3 tablespoons sunflower oil
$^{1}/_{2}$ teaspoon Dijon mustard
$^{1}/_{2}$ teaspoon crushed garlic
dash of pepper and salt

Method
Place mixed beans in a bowl, pour boiling water over them, and allow them to soak overnight. Next day, pour off the water, place the beans in a saucepan, and cover with cold water. Bring to the boil and simmer for about 1 hour. Drain and leave aside to cool.

Place the beans and seasoning in a salad bowl, and mix well. Add the dressing and stir it all together. Chill until required.

Method for dressing
Chop the mint with a scissors. Pop it in a screw-top jar and add the rest of the dressing ingredients. Shake, shake, shake.

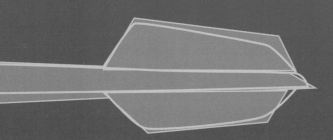

tomatoes with buffalo mozzarella and basil

Serves **4**

Ingredients
4 medium tomatoes
4 slices buffalo mozzarella
4 torn basil leaves

Dressing
3 tablespoons olive oil
1 tablespoon red wine vinegar
$^1/_4$ teaspoon Dijon mustard
pepper and salt
$^1/_2$ teaspoon crushed garlic

Method
Cut a cross on top of the tomatoes, place them in a bowl and pour boiling water over them. Allow them to sit for 3 minutes, then pour off the hot water and add cold water. Now peel off the skin. Dry the tomatoes and cut into medium slices. Place in a serving bowl. Add sliced mozzarella and scatter torn basil leaves on top. Pour some of the dressing on top and serve the rest separately. Simple but tasty.

Method for dressing
Shake in a jar or whisk in a jug.

leafy lardons with orange and walnut dressing

Serves ❹

Ingredients

Croutons
2 slices white sliced pan
1 tablespoon olive oil
1 clove garlic, crushed
1 tablespoon grated Parmesan cheese

Lardons
4 smoked streaky rashers (rinds removed and cut into strips)
1 dessertspoon olive oil

Salad
1 bag assorted salad leaves (pre-washed)

50 g (2 oz) feta cheese, cut into cubes (optional)
4 cherry tomatoes

Dressing
3 dessertspoons freshly squeezed orange juice
1 teaspoon lemon juice
1 teaspoon grated orange rind (Grate this before cutting for the juice)
6 dessertspoons olive oil
3 dessertspoons sunflower oil
$^1/_2$ teaspoon grain mustard
1 dessertspoon chopped walnuts
1 teaspoon runny honey
pepper and salt

Method

To make the croutons, place the bread on a chopping board and remove the crusts. Now cut into cubes. Put the cubed bread on a baking tray. Mix with olive oil, crushed garlic and Parmesan cheese. Place in a moderate oven (140°–160°C/275°–315°F/gas mark 4–6) and allow to become golden—approximately 10 minutes. Allow to cool, and place aside.

Method for lardons

Place streaky rashers on chopping board. Remove rind with a knife or scissors. Cut into narrow strips. Heat olive oil in a frying pan. Add the bacon and fry until crisp. Remove to kitchen pepper and allow to cool.

To assemble salad

Divide lettuce leaves between four dinner plates. Scatter lardons, croutons and feta cheese (if using) all around. Top with cherry tomatoes and pour dressing over or serve separately.

Method for dressing

Mix all the ingredients in a screw-top jar and shake well, or place all the ingredients in a jug and whisk with a fork.

fruity cous cous

Serves **4**

Ingredients
2 cups cous cous
2 cups boiling water
4 dried apricots
1 red eating apple
1 orange
8 blueberries
4 medium strawberries
4 green grapes
4 dark grapes

Dressing
1 tablespoon freshly squeezed orange juice
3 tablespoons sunflower oil
$^1/_2$ teaspoon Dijon mustard
pepper and salt

Method
Place cous cous in a bowl. Pour boiling water over it and allow to sit for 5 or 6 minutes or until all the liquid is absorbed. Fork through. Chop the dried apricots into small pieces. Wipe the apple—do not peel—and cut into small pieces. Peel the orange and divide into segments. Leave the blueberries whole. Wipe the strawberries and cut into quarters. Deseed the grapes (or, better still, try to get seedless ones). Add to cous cous and mix well.

Method for dressing
Put all the dressing ingredients together in a screw-top jar or jug and shake well. Pour over the cous cous and mix through. What a gorgeous dish to serve!

thai chicken with bean sprouts and noodles

Serves ❹

Ingredients

4 chicken breasts (uncooked)
1 cup bean sprouts
1 pack medium egg noodles
to garnish: **coriander leaves**

Marinade
2 teaspoons soy sauce
2 teaspoons runny honey
3 tablespoons sunflower oil
1 teaspoon crushed garlic

Dressing
2 tablespoons lime juice
$^1/_2$ teaspoon fish sauce
6 tablespoons sunflower oil
1 teaspoon chopped coriander
1 teaspoon grain mustard
salt and pepper

Method

Mix all the ingredients for the marinade together in a bowl. Add the chicken breasts and mix well. Cover with cling film and place in the fridge for at least 1 hour, or overnight if possible. Line a baking tray with tin foil and place the marinated chicken on it. Cover this with another layer of tin foil and cook in the oven at 170°C (325°F/gas mark 5) for approximately 25 minutes. Allow to cool. To cook the noodles, place them in a bowl, pour boiling water over them, and allow them to stand for 5 minutes, then drain and mix them with the bean sprouts.

To serve

Arrange the noodles and bean sprouts on a large plate. Slice the chicken breast into strips and place on top. Garnish with coriander leaves.

Method for dressing

Make dressing by mixing all the ingredients together in a screw-top jar or jug. Pour over the chicken and noodles or serve separately.

adzuki bean salad with honey and balsamic dressing

Serves **4**

Ingredients
1 cup adzuki beans
3 cm (1¹/₄ in) long piece of root ginger, peeled and chopped
1 tablespoon sultanas
pepper and salt

Dressing
1 tablespoon balsamic vinegar
3 tablespoons olive oil
1 teaspoon runny honey
¹/₂ teaspoon grain mustard
tip of a teaspoon of creamed garlic

Method
Soak the beans for 4 hours in a bowl. Pour into a saucepan and simmer for 10 minutes. Drain and allow to cool.

Mix the beans, ginger, sultanas and seasoning together. Add the dressing and stir through. Serve in a fancy dish.

Method for dressing
Make the dressing by mixing all the ingredients together in a screw-top jar or jug.

chow salad

Serves **4**

Ingredients
2 cups white cabbage (shredded)
1 teaspoon oregano
black pepper

Dressing
1 cup natural yoghurt
1 tablespoon white wine vinegar
¹/₂ teaspoon Dijon mustard
¹/₂ teaspoon crushed garlic
1 teaspoon sesame seeds
pepper and salt

Method
To shred the cabbage, place half a head of hard white cabbage on a chopping board, and slice thinly with a large knife. Place the shredded cabbage in a bowl. Add oregano and a few twists of black pepper. Mix all the ingredients for the dressing together in a screw-top jar and add to the cabbage mixture. Stir well through the cabbage. Place in a serving dish and chill until required.

wild rice, red pepper and prawn salad

Serves **4**

Ingredients
1 cup cooked prawns
2 cups cooked wild rice
1 small red pepper
2 spring onions
$^1/_2$ teaspoon paprika pepper
$^1/_2$ teaspoon dry mustard
pepper and salt

Dressing
1 dessertspoon chopped mint
1 dessertspoon white wine vinegar
2 dessertspoons fresh orange juice
6 dessertspoons sunflower oil
dash of Tabasco

Method
If using Dublin Bay prawn tails, place in a saucepan, cover with boiling water and simmer for 5 minutes. Drain, allow to cool, and remove the shells.

Place the wild rice in a saucepan. Cover with cold water, bring to the boil and simmer gently for approximately 40 minutes. Strain and run the cold tap through to wash away any sticky substance. Drain well and place in a bowl. Slice and chop the red pepper and add to the rice. Remove the base from the spring onions, wipe, cut into small pieces, and add to the rice. Add prawns, paprika, mustard and seasoning. Mix well. Add the dressing, stirring it into the mixture. Place in a serving bowl and chill.

Method for dressing
Place all the ingredients in a screw-top jar or a jug and mix well.

green lentil and wild rice salad

Serves **4**

Ingredients
1¹/₂ cups green lentils (available in health-food shops)
1¹/₂ cups wild rice
¹/₂ cup chopped red pepper, deseeded and stalks removed
¹/₂ cup chopped yellow pepper, deseeded and stalks removed
pepper and salt
to serve: a little chopped coriander (optional)

Dressing
2 tablespoons lime juice
6 tablespoons sunflower oil
1 teaspoon grain mustard
1 teaspoon crushed garlic

Method
Place the green lentils in a saucepan, cover with cold water, bring to the boil and simmer for approximately 40 minutes or until tender. Strain through a colander and leave aside.

Place the rice in a saucepan, cover with cold water, bring to the boil and simmer for 40 minutes. Strain through a colander and leave aside to cool.

Mix lentils, rice and peppers together in a bowl. Mix all the dressing ingredients together in a screw-top jar or jug. Pour the dressing over the rice mixture, add pepper and salt, and mix well. Stir in a little chopped coriander, if desired. Divide into four small bowls or leave in a large bowl.

parma ham and baby leaf salad

Serves **4**

Ingredients

$^1/_2$ **head oak leaf lettuce**
3 cups lamb's lettuce
4 slices Parma ham per person
5 tablespoons extra virgin olive oil
4 tablespoons good-quality balsamic vinegar (e.g. Romanico)
fresh Parmesan cheese
black pepper
croutons (optional)

Method

Tear the lettuce with your hands if the leaves are going to be too large to bite. Wash in a colander and drain on kitchen paper. Pat dry. Arrange the leaves decoratively on each plate. Prepare the ham by slicing each slice into three. Roll each piece up and place on the plate. Put the vinegar and oil together in a jug and pour on top. Using the largest pull on your grater, grate the fresh Parmesan on top. Twist a little black pepper on top. Add croutons, if desired.

Fruity cous cous

Thai chicken with bean sprouts
and noodles

Red ripe berry salad

Wild rice, red pepper
and prawn salad

Fillet steak and beetroot salad

9

a bit
on the
side

sweet sauces

caramel sauce

Under adult supervision

Ingredients
3 tablespoons sugar
3 tablespoons cold water
3 tablespoons hot water

Method
Place sugar and cold water in a small saucepan and allow to dissolve over a low heat.
Bring to the boil and simmer for approximately 10 minutes until a golden caramel colour is
reached.

Remove from the heat, stand back a little, and add the hot water. Allow to boil up and
simmer for 2 minutes. Be careful—it will be very hot! Allow to cool and serve cold with
chosen dessert.

quick chocolate sauce

Ingredients
50 g (2 oz) cooking chocolate (broken into pieces)
125 ml (¹/₄ pint) water
1 dessertspoon cream (optional)

Method
Place chocolate and water in a small saucepan. Stir over a low heat until chocolate has dissolved. Simmer for approximately 5 minutes or until the sauce coats the back of a spoon. Pour into a sauceboat and serve hot.

fruit coulis

Most soft fruits can be used. Raspberries, strawberries and mangoes are most popular.

Ingredients
1 cup raspberries or mango chunks
¹/₃ cup water
¹/₃ cup sugar

Method
Place fruit in a small saucepan with water and sugar. Bring to the boil and simmer for approximately 4 minutes or until fruit is soft. Place in a liquidiser and process until smooth.

Use for decorating plates with your selected dessert.

For strawberries, place 1 cup of sliced strawberries in the processor and 1 tablespoon of icing sugar and process until smooth.

savoury sauces & dressings

mint pesto

Basil pesto is in the starters section (see page 62)

Ingredients
1 cup fresh mint leaves
1 dessertspoon grilled walnuts or pistachios with the skin rubbed off
1 dessertspoon grated Parmesan cheese
$^1/_2$ teaspoon crushed garlic
$^1/_2$ cup olive oil

Method
Place all the ingredients **except** the oil in a food processor or liquidiser. Blend for a minute or until everything is chopped.

Add the olive oil and switch on again for 1 minute until well blended. Use straightaway or place in a screw-top jar and use within 2 days.

basic vinaigrette dressing

Ingredients
1 tablespoon red wine vinegar
3 tablespoons olive oil
pepper and salt
¹/₂ teaspoon Dijon mustard
A teaspoon of runny honey may be added or ¹/₂ teaspoon crushed garlic, if desired

Method
Place all the ingredients in a jar with a lid and shake well. This dressing will keep in the fridge for 10 days.

Remember: No matter how much you are making, it is always 1 part vinegar to 3 parts oil.

blue balsamic sauce

Ingredients
1 cup blueberries
1 tablespoon sugar
1 tablespoon balsamic vinegar
1 tablespoon tomato ketchup
¹/₂ teaspoon creamed garlic

Method
Place all the ingredients in a saucepan, mix well and bring to simmer for a few minutes. Liquidise and use as required.

dill dressing

Ingredients

3 tablespoons sunflower oil
1 tablespoon white wine vinegar
1 teaspoon chopped fresh dill
$^1/_2$ teaspoon Dalkey or any other grain mustard
$^1/_4$ teaspoon honey

Method
Place all ingredients in a screw-top jar and shake well.

barbecue sauce

Ingredients

3 dessertspoons tomato ketchup
1 dessertspoon red wine vinegar
1 teaspoon honey
$^1/_3$ teaspoon crushed garlic
1 dessertspoon vegetable oil
pinch of salt and pepper
$^1/_3$ teaspoon Dalkey or another grain mustard

Method
Mix all the ingredients together well in a bowl or jar.

tomato sauce

Ingredients

1 small onion, finely chopped

1 clove garlic (creamed or crushed)

1 dessertspoon chopped basil

$^1/_2$ tin chopped tomatoes

1 tablespoon olive oil

seasoning—salt and pepper

a squirt of tomato purée

Method

On a chopping board, finely slice the onion, then prepare the garlic. Chop the basil using a scissors. Open the tin of tomatoes.

Heat the olive oil in a saucepan and add the finely chopped onions and garlic. Sauté for a few minutes, then add the chopped tomatoes and pureé, basil and seasoning. Simmer for a few minutes until mixed well. This can be liquidised if a smoother sause is required. Pour over pasta, such as cannelloni.

béchamel sauce (quick basic white sauce)

Ingredients

25 g (1 oz) butter

25 g (1 oz) flour

250 ml (9 fl oz) milk

pepper and salt

Method

Place the butter and flour in a small saucepan. Place over a moderate heat and allow the butter to melt, stirring continually. Remove from heat and add in the milk, slowly. Use a small whisk to whisk away the lumps. Return to the heat and stir well with a wooden spoon. Allow to simmer for 5 minutes. Season.

A dessertspoon of chopped parsley may be added to make it into parsley sauce.

To make it into a cheese sauce, 2 dessertspoons of grated red cheddar cheese may be added.

thai dressing

Ingredients
$1/2$ **red chilli**
1 teaspoon chopped root ginger
$1/2$ **teaspoon brown sugar**
$1/2$ **teaspoon crushed garlic**
3 tablespoons lime juice
3 tablespoons olive oil
1 tablespoon sesame oil
1 tablespoon fish sauce (nam pla)
1 tablespoon chopped coriander
pepper and salt

Method
Place the red chilli on a chopping board and cut in two. Remove the stalk and seeds and chop finely. Place in a jug. Peel and chop the ginger. Add the ginger and brown sugar to the jug with the chilli. Crush a clove of garlic or enough to fill a teaspoon and pop this into the jug. Squeeze the lime and pour in the required amount. Add the olive and sesame oil and fish sauce and stir well. Finely chop some fresh coriander and add this to the jug, along with salt and pepper. Mix well.

In Thai cooking, fish sauce (nam pla) is used in the same way as soy sauce is used in Chinese cooking. It doesn't smell the best but it adds a delicious flavour and the smell quickly evaporates.

Here's an unusual dressing we picked up on our culinary travels.

balsamic syrup dressing

Ingredients
2 teaspoons brown sugar
125 ml (4¹/₂ fl oz) water
1 tablespoon balsamic vinegar

Method
Place sugar and water in a small saucepan and allow the sugar to dissolve over a low heat. When they are dissolved, add the balsamic vinegar and stand back. Bring to the boil and allow to simmer for 3 minutes. Serve hot or cold.

1 teaspoon of port may be added before the balsamic vinegar if this dressing is to be served to adults.

blue cheese dressing

Ingredients
100 g (4 oz) blue cheese (e.g. stilton or Cashel blue)
2 tablespoons mayonnaise
1 tablespoon cream
1 tablespoon white wine vinegar
salt and pepper to taste

Method
Place the blue cheese on a plate and mash with a fork. Mix mayonnaise, cream and white wine vinegar in a jug or bowl. Add the mashed blue cheese and mix well until all the ingredients are combined. Add pepper and salt to taste. Go easy on the salt as some blue cheeses are quite salty on their own.

This dressing goes well in a salad with croutons.

croutons

Ingredients
4 slices white bread
1 tablespoon olive oil
$^1/_2$ clove garlic, crushed
1 tablespoon freshly grated Parmesan cheese

Method
Cut the crusts off the bread and cut the slices into small cubes. Place on a baking tray and sprinkle with olive oil, a little crushed garlic and a sprinkle of Parmesan cheese. Pop in a moderate oven (140°–160°C/275°–315°F/gas mark 4–5) and bake until crisp and slightly golden. Cool on some kitchen paper and store in an airtight container.

shoppers' guide to farmers' markets

Farmers' markets have spread like wildfire around the country. Full of the freshest ingredients and unusual finds, they are a must visit for every avid chef. The diversity is splendid. You can buy everything from antiques to olive oil. Check out your local market on our tasty list below. Most run from June through till September each year. This is the new way to shop for the freshest ingredients. From the seed to the feed!

ANTRIM
Belfast, St George's Street—Saturday
Lisburn—Saturday

ARMAGH
Portadown—last Saturday of month

CARLOW
Carlow town—potato market, Saturday, 9 a.m. to 2 p.m.

CLARE
Ballyvaughan—Thursday, 10 a.m. to 2 p.m.
Ennis—Friday, 8 a.m. to 2 p.m.
Killaloe—Sunday, 11 a.m. to 3 p.m.
Kilrush, on the square—Saturday, 10 a.m. to 2 p.m.

CORK CITY
Cornmarket Street—Saturday 9 a.m. to 1.30 p.m.
Douglas, community park—Saturday
The English Market—every day

CORK COUNTY
Ballincollig—Friday, 10 a.m.

Ballydehob—Friday, 10.30 a.m. to 12 noon
Bandon—Friday, 10.30 a.m. to 1 p.m.
Bantry—Friday, 9 a.m. to 1 p.m.
Blackwatervalley—fortnightly, Saturday
Castletownbere—first Thursday of month
Clonakilty—Thursday and Saturday, 10 a.m. to 2 p.m.
Cobh, sea front—Friday, 10 a.m. to 1 p.m.
Dunmanway—Friday, 10 a.m. to 2 p.m.
Fermoy—Saturday; Fermoy Country Market—Friday afternoon
Inchigeelagh—last Saturday of month
Kanturk—Saturday 10.30 a.m. to 12.30 p.m.
Killavullen—fortnightly, Saturday
Macroom—Tuesdays, 9 a.m. to 4 p.m.
Mallow—country market, Saturday 9 a.m. to 1 p.m.
Midleton Farmers' Market—Saturday, 10 a.m. to 2 p.m.
Mitchelstown, town square—Saturday
Schull—June–September, Sunday, 11 a.m. to 3 p.m.
Skibbereen—Saturday, 9 a.m. to 1.30 p.m.

DONEGAL
Donegal town, the Diamond—one Saturday a month
Letterkenny—first and third Saturday of month

DOWN
Templepatrick—one Sunday a month

DUBLIN
Dalkey—Friday, 10 a.m. to 4 p.m.
Dublin Docklands—Docklands Market, Thursday, 10 a.m. to 3 p.m.
Dundrum—Saturday, 10 a.m. to 4 p.m.
Dún Laoghaire—Harbour Market, Saturday, 10 a.m. to 4 p.m.; People's Park Market, Sunday, 11 a.m. to 4 p.m.

Leopardstown Racecourse Market—Friday,
11 a.m. to 6 p.m.
Malahide—Saturday, 10 a.m. to 4 p.m.
Marlay Park—Saturday, 10 a.m. to 4 p.m.
Monkstown Village Market—Saturday, 10 a.m.
to 4 p.m.
Pearse Street Market—Saturday, 9.30 a.m. to
3 p.m.
Ranelagh—Sunday, 10 a.m. to 4 p.m.
Rush, Fingal Arts Centre—last Sunday of month
Sandycove—Cavistons Food Emporium—
01 2809120
Temple Bar Food Market—Saturday morning
and Wednesday, 11 a.m. to 3 p.m.
Wolfe Tone Park—gourmet food market, Friday,
11 a.m. to 3 p.m.

GALWAY
Galway, beside St Nicholas's Church, Saturday
morning

KERRY
Caherdaniel—Friday, 10 a.m. to 12 noon
Cahirciveen—Thursday, 11 a.m. to 2 p.m.
Dingle—Friday, 10 a.m. to 4 p.m.
Kenmare, Bridge Street—Wednesday-Sunday,
10 a.m. to 6 p.m.
Killarney—country market, Friday, 11.30 a.m. to
1.30 p.m.
Killorglin, CYMS hall—Friday, 11 a.m. to 1 p.m.
Listowel—food fair, Thursday, 10 a.m. to 1 p.m.
Milltown—organic market, Saturday, 10 a.m. to
2 p.m.
Sneem—Tuesday, 11 a.m. to 2 p.m.
Tralee—Friday, 9 a.m. to 5 p.m.

KILDARE
Athy, Sunday, 10 a.m. to 3 p.m.
Kildare Folly Market, every third Sunday
Naas—Saturday,10 a.m. to 3 p.m.

KILKENNY
First and third Sunday of month

LIMERICK
Abbeyfeale, parish hall—Friday, 9 a.m. to 1 p.m.
Limerick City—Milk Market, Saturday, 8 a.m. to
2 p.m.

LONGFORD
none known at present

LOUTH
Castle Bellingham—first Sunday of month,
11 a.m. to 6 p.m.
Dundalk, at the museum
Kilcock—Larchill market, third Sunday of month,
11 a.m. to 6 p.m.

MEATH
Clonee, the gardenworks—food market,
Saturday, 10 a.m. to 3 p.m.
Enfield—Friday
Kells—Saturday 10 a.m. to 2 p.m.
Oldcastle—Friday

OFFALY
Birr—the Full Moon Market, every third Saturday
Tullamore, Millennium Square—Saturday, 9 a.m.
to 4 p.m.

TIPPERARY
Cahir, beside craft granary yard—9 a.m. to
1 p.m.

TYRONE
none known at present

WATERFORD
Dungarven, Scanlon's car park—Thursday, 9.30
a.m. to 2 p.m.
Dunhill, parish hall—last Sunday of month,
11.30 a.m. to 1 p.m.
Waterford, Jenkins Lane—Saturday, 10 a.m. to
4 p.m.

WESTMEATH
Mullingar—Sunday

WEXFORD
Campile, New Ross, Dunbrody Abbey Centre—
Sunday 12 to 3.30 p.m.
Enniscorthy—Saturday, 9 a.m. to 2 p.m.

WICKLOW
Arklow—Saturday, 10.10 a.m. to 12 noon
Avoca—July and August, Sunday
Blessington—Saturday, 2.30 to 4.30 p.m.
Glendalough—second Sunday of month,
11 a.m. to 4 p.m.
Kilcoole—Saturday, 10.30 to 11.30 a.m.
Macreddin village—Brooklodge market, first and
third Sunday of month
Kilpeddar—Marc Michel, Organic Life Market
and Restaurant—01 2011882
Powerscourt, car park next to waterfall—second
and fourth Sunday of month
Roundwood—Sunday, 3 to 5 p.m.

If your town is not mentioned, try looking
up www.irelandmarkets.com

Index

tomatoes with buffalo mozzarella and
basil, 176
mughal: chicken mughal and wild rice, 88
mushrooms, 23
aubergine and mushroom kebabs, 155
black-eyed beans with mushroom and Thai
green sauce, 153
garlic mushrooms, 151
mushroom and seafood quiche, 84
stuffed mushrooms, 39
vol-au-vents with chicken and mushroom in
creamy tarragon sauce, 60–1
mussels: crunchy garlic mussels, 55
mustard, 23
honey and mustard salad dressing, 51

nachos, chilli, 76
New England lemonade, 144
noodles, 23–4
chicken coconut curry with noodles, 68
Oriental pork with noodles, 78
posh pitta stir-fry, 157
nuts, 24 see also individual nuts

oaties: Eve's oaties, 123
oils, 24–5
omelette, Spanish, 149
onions, 25
brochette of lamb, red onion and
aubergine, 94–5
red onion marmalade, 57
roasted red onion broccoli tart, 69
oranges, 25
orange and walnut salad dressing, 177
rhubarb, orange and ginger crumble, 101
oregano, 33
Oriental pork with noodles, 78
oven temperatures, 20, 21, 23
pre-heating, 27

paella: veggie paella, 154
pan-fried fillet of lemon sole with citrus
butter, 85
papaya, 35
paprika, 25
chicken paprika, 80
Parma ham and baby leaf salad, 184
parmesan cheese, 25
parsley, 33
parsnips
curried parsnip and apple soup, 162

veggie chips, 156
passion fruit, 35
pasta, 25–6
beef cannelloni with tomato sauce, 91
buttons and bows, 61
fettuccini with creamy garlic and bacon
sauce, 81
pasta pesto, 62
pasta salad with char-grilled chicken, 51
pasta with herbs, garlic and olive oil, 72
spinach and ricotta cannelloni, 89
sweet pepper penne, 82
pastry, 26
choux pastry, 104
pâté
aubergine pâté, 53
fresh salmon pâté, 48
smoked mackerel pâté, 40
peaches, 26
peanut butter, 138
peanut butter cookies, 117
peanut butter sauce, 46, 155
yellow nutter smoothie, 138
pears, 26
chocolate and pear crumble, 100
peas, 26–7
pecan nuts, 24
chocolate pecan pie, 115
penne: sweet pepper penne, 82
peppercorns, 27
peppers, 27
Mediterranean vegetables, 93
stuffed green peppers with ratatouille, 148
sweet pepper penne, 82
sweet red pepper soup, 161
veggie paella, 154
wild rice, red pepper and prawn salad, 182
pesto, 62
mint pesto, 190
pesto mayonnaise, 157
physalis, 35
pies and tarts
apple tart, 103
chocolate pecan pie, 115
pilaff rice, 86
pineapples, 27, 142
pina co-ladmad smoothie, 142
pine nuts
celeriac and pine nut soup, 165
grilled guacamole nests with prawn and pine
nut centre, 45

Win a cookery class with Bee herself!

This is your opportunity to win a one off chance to learn to prepare and cook a tasty three-course meal with Bee Walsh.

Bee has been involved in teaching young people how to cook for many years, both at the Busy Bee School of cookery and in various secondary schools.
The prize is a cookery session in which you will learn to prepare, cook and enjoy a three-course meal on a one-to-one basis.

1 To enter the competition, answer the following question:

   What does DVD stand for in this book?

2 Fill in your details and post this page to:
   The Right Bite Competition, Gill & Macmillan, Hume Avenue, Park West, Dublin 12

   Name:

   Address:

   Daytime telephone number:

3 This entry does not give rise to any contract between Gill & Macmillan Ltd. ('Gill & Macmillan') and the entrant.

4 The competition will be run and determined in accordance with the Rules below.

RULES

1. The instructions above form part of the Rules.
2. Only entries on an original entry form contained at the end of a copy of *The Right Bite* will be considered.
3. All entries must be received by Gill & Macmillan prior to, or not later than, 30 November 2006 ('the Closing Date').
4. Gill & Macmillan reserves the right to extend the Closing Date if necessary.
5. Multiple entries will be accepted.
6. No cash will be offered in lieu of the prize available in the competition.
7. Gill & Macmillan will, in its absolute discretion, decide any matter or question concerning the running of the competition. These Rules, their interpretation or any ancillary matter and any

such decision or necessary opinion of Gill & Macmillan will be final and no correspondence will be entered into concerning such a decision.
8. Gill & Macmillan will notify the winner within 30 days of the Closing Date that he/she has been successful.
9. Gill & Macmillan will have no responsibility for, and is not obliged to take into account, any entry lost, damaged or delayed in the post or otherwise.
10. All entries must be sent and received by Gill & Macmillan, by ordinary post. Entries received by any means other than ordinary post such as by hand, courier, facsimilie, etc. will not be accepted or considered.

11. The competition is open to residents of the Republic of Ireland, except the author, employees of Gill & Macmillan and their families, and employees and/or administration of Busy Bee Cookery School and this competition.
12. The winner's name may, at Gill & Macmillan's discretion, be used for publicity purposes.
13. The value of this prize does not exceed €1,000. Prize includes cookery class for one person. Gill & Macmillan and Busy Bee Cookery School are free from any liability involved in travel to/from and participation in the prize.